Navigating
YOUR WAY TO
BUSINESS
SUCCESS

Navigating YOUR WAY TO BUSINESS SUCCESS

An Entrepreneur's JOURNEY

KATHRYN B. FREELAND MBA

Foreword by Dr. Freeman A. Hrabowski III

FreeBridge Publishing, Inc.

Pasadena, Maryland

Published by
FreeBridge Publishing, Inc.
Pasadena, Maryland

Publisher's Cataloging-in-Publication Data
Freeland, Kathryn B.

    Navigating your way to business success : an entrepreneur's journey
    / Kathryn B. Freeland. – Pasadena, Md. : FreeBridge Pub., Inc., 2009.

    p. ; cm.

    ISBN: 978-0-9823578-0-4

    1. Success in business. I. Title.

    HF5386.F74 2009
    650.1—dc22   2009923125

Project coordination by Jenkins Group, Inc.
www.BookPublishing.com
Design by Yvonne Fetig Roehler

FIRST EDITION

Printed in the United States of America
13 12 11 10 09 • 5 4 3 2 1

DEDICATION

This book is dedicated to

the memory of my father,
Junior D. Bridges;

Betty T. Wooten, my dear friend
who succumbed to breast cancer in January 2009;

and to my dear friend and trusted advisor
Chris Parrotta, the former CFO of RGII Technologies Inc.
Chris died on January 29, 2009,
the day after commenting on what photo
to use on the cover of the book.

I will forever have a void in my life,
for each of them impacted me
intellectually, emotionally, and spiritually.
They all journeyed to heaven
before this book was completed,
but they all will live on in my memories.

CONTENTS

FOREWORD

If you ask most Americans to name three successful African American women entrepreneurs, the first, of course, would be Oprah Winfrey, and those who know something about black history would likely mention Madam C. J. Walker. But many would be hard-pressed to name a third—especially if we ask about entrepreneurs in technology. We know that a substantial gap exists between minority-owned businesses and businesses overall in America. In fact, while minorities represent nearly one-third of the U.S. population, they own only 18% of all businesses, including 5% black owned. Moreover, women own only 28% of all businesses, with African American women representing just 2% of all business owners.

Anyone who meets Kathy Freeland immediately senses the rare combination of self-confidence and humility, in addition to an aura of somehow being more experienced and wiser than her youthful appearance immediately suggests. When I first began talking with her several years ago, I was fascinated by this impressive businesswoman who had come to Maryland from the Deep South. It was clear that she was well educated, thoughtful, and deliberate in her thinking about building relationships with others. It wasn't too long before I began to learn her story: from growing up in Birmingham (my hometown) in a deeply religious, working-class family and coming to the Washington, D.C., area to work as a program analyst at a government-contractor company to deciding to start her own company and overcoming all sorts of odds and succeeding as a visionary and pioneer in the world of technology.

As she and I talked about her potential involvement with my campus, I could not help but notice how she already understood the university's position in the state of Maryland and how thoughtful her questions were about my vision as a leader, our values as an institution, and our challenges. It did not take long to understand that she was someone who lived and breathed the American dream, who understood the power of education to transform lives, who not only had experienced spectacular success but also, even more important, who was determined to contribute to others' success. She wanted to know about the needs of the university and our students and about our relationships with the corporate community. She was determined to understand what we were doing to help women and minorities. She was particularly intrigued by our Center for Women and Information Technology (CWIT) and our entrepreneurship activities involving incubator and postincubator companies in biotechnology and information technology. Since those initial meetings, Kathy and her husband, Greg, have been enormously generous to our campus, with their time, helping to recruit students, hiring our students to be interns, and serving as mentors.

As we have worked to encourage greater diversity among students interested in entrepreneurship, her involvement with the university has been important in the university's entrepreneurial activities. Students of all races benefit from learning about the success stories of minority entrepreneurs, and faculty can use the stories of these businesspeople in their teaching—all of which makes our thinking about entrepreneurship more inclusive of all Americans.

Kathy clearly understands the important role that universities will play in producing Americans who have the skills and preparation to start companies and to build innovation in America—and this is why it is so critical that we have successful entrepreneurs reflecting on their experiences and helping others understand the kinds of questions and approaches that one must use to ensure success.

Navigating Your Way to Business Success is an enlightened chronicle of an unusual entrepreneur and goes a long way toward showing all of us— especially potential entrepreneurs, whether students, employees, or company owners—what it takes to be a successful entrepreneur. What makes the book so compelling is the author's authenticity. Having known Kathy for a decade, I am not surprised that she would be willing to share with others both her personal story and lessons learned through her professional career. The book begins with a moment of disappointment, when she is overlooked for a promotion she deserves and has to train someone else whom she considers less prepared for the job. Many readers will easily relate to that experience. She writes about the importance of supportive relationships—of having people in her life, like her husband and friends, who listened to her frustration and gave her support as she thought about a backup plan while continuing to do her work.

The approach she takes in the book is exactly the approach she has taken in her career: engaging, step by step, in extensive research and careful analysis, with a strong emphasis on developing the right questions and considerable focus on experiences. As is true in getting to know Kathy, the reader will be inspired by her ability to weave a story based on facts and reflection—from losing a child and experiencing cancer to growing and then selling a business. Her spirit of risk taking, based on careful assessment and unusual curiosity, comes through over and over. Just as she knows how to build a relationship with a customer, she skillfully connects to readers by telling them what she is going to talk about; giving them specific, concrete examples to make her point; addressing potential obstacles and challenges they may face; and providing a variety of tools and resources they may use (from the Small Business Development Centers and the Service Corps of Retired Executives to using technology in all aspects of the business development process). When Kathy talks about the importance of a business plan, she does so because she believes so strongly in doing her homework, building strong relationships, being well qualified, understanding the particular industry, knowing competitors, relying on a variety of experts, and hiring and supporting the most talented people.

Carl Schramm, president and CEO of the Kauffman Foundation, which supports many of my university's and many others' efforts to infuse entrepreneurship throughout the curriculum, from the arts to engineering, suggests the following in his book The Entrepreneurial Imperative: "The Entrepreneurial Society envisions that all Americans have an entrepreneurial role to play, that they understand the process and the importance of innovation and personal creativity and the legitimacy of business as an outlet for human potential." Moreover, "the nation must help identify, recruit, coach, and support minority business people who have technology skills and the ability to build sizable new businesses."

There is no doubt that Freeland's story will inspire many women, African Americans, and others to consider for themselves the possibility of entrepreneurship. All of us need to see people like ourselves who have achieved their dreams. And when successful people tell us not only about their achievements but also about their challenges, we can see ourselves in them and believe that obstacles, both personal and professional, can be overcome and that dreams do not have to be deferred forever.

What we derive from knowing Kathy Freeland and her story is the sense that she knows who she is, that she is proud of her strong faith, that she constantly takes the time not only to prepare but also to act and then learn from her actions—both the successes and the setbacks—and to look her future squarely in the eye. Throughout her remarkable story, we see a businesswoman who understands the importance of preparation, innovation, and constant analysis, even as she thinks about the timing of her decision to sell her company and the pros and cons of that decision-making process. We also can tell that she is using lessons learned over the past two decades to prepare for the next phase of her life. Those of us who know her have no doubt that, notwithstanding her already spectacular American journey, the best is yet to come.

Dr. Freeman A. Hrabowski III
President
University of Maryland, Baltimore County

ACKNOWLEDGMENTS

To all aspiring entrepreneurs who question whether entrepreneurship is for you: I'm living proof that, yes, it can be done, and, yes, you can achieve success through business ownership, even when the odds are stacked against you.

To Marcia Turner, who helped me to write my first book, I am grateful for your patience, guidance, opinions, and openness throughout this process. Your calming spirit helped me stay focused when I couldn't find the right words. We make a good team.

To the staff and my project coordinators at Jenkins Group, Inc., Leah Nicholson, Yvonne Roehler, and Jerry Jenkins, thanks for your instructional and informative guidance and gentle pushes to keep me on my own self-imposed schedule. You taught me more about book publishing than I would have ever learned on my own.

Last, to my family, the loves of my life: Greg, Brya, and Brynn. God has blessed me abundantly, but the greatest blessing is having each of you in my life. Without your love and support, I could not have made this journey. I love you more than words can say, and I am grateful that you love me unconditionally.

CHAPTER 1

MAKING THE DECISION TO BECOME YOUR OWN BOSS

"And the Lord shall make thee the head, and not the tail;
and thou shalt be above only, and thou shalt not be beneath."
— Deuteronomy 28:13

A s my boss stepped into my office, I knew that I was about to be named my company's new program supervisor. Two years earlier, in 1990, I had been hired as program analyst at a small government contractor outside Washington, D.C., and had quickly stepped up to every task given to me, resulting in a promotion to program manager. Soon, I was one of the senior team members supporting the firm's government clients.

In truth, I had been acting as supervisor, supported by my boss, for several months. I had the tenure, the experience, and the knowledge of the job, so it was almost a foregone conclusion that I would be officially named as her replacement.

She was moving on, and the company had invited internal candidates to apply, which I did, although I knew they also had to evaluate candidates on the outside to make the hiring process look fair. But I also knew it was unnecessary. No one else was better suited to this position. I was sure of it, my colleagues were sure of it, and I was fairly certain my boss was sure of it.

So, the moment had arrived, and I was almost bursting with anticipation and excitement. Finally, the promotion I deserved!

"Kathy, a decision has been made about my replacement," my boss told me, "and the company has selected one of the other candidates."

The expectant smile on my face slowly faded as the words sunk in, though it took a few minutes for the message to register. I didn't get the job? For once in my life, I was speechless. How could I *not* have gotten the job? In my mind, I had it in the bag. What had happened?

After some time, I managed to ask, "Who got the position, and why wasn't it me?"

"A candidate outside the company had significantly more experience," she explained.

The rest of the day was a blur as I grappled with this new information. How could someone outside the company have been deemed a better fit for this position when I had been doing the work—and doing it well—for months? I had the direct experience working on these programs and the knowledge of and relationship with the customers. How could that not have been enough? I repeated her words over and over in my mind, trying to force my brain to understand and accept them. It wasn't working.

My colleagues were just as shocked as I was, though certainly not as disappointed. No one could have been as let down as I was at not receiving the promotion. Although I continued to come to work, the disillusionment I felt tainted my attitude toward my employer. The company had let me down badly, and for the first time, I felt discriminated against.

THE BEGINNING OF THE END OF MY LIFE AS AN EMPLOYEE

My new boss, a man only two years my senior, came on board almost immediately to transition into his new role as my former boss prepared to leave. To my chagrin, I was asked to train him. The request made sense because I had been doing the work and was most familiar with the requirements of the job, but it also highlighted the ridiculousness of the hiring decision. Why hadn't they simply promoted me?

I replayed this question again and again in my mind as I continued to explain the intricacies of the job to my new *boss*, who lacked direct experience and relationships with the actual customer and the actual programs. To his credit, he did have several years of business/government contract experience. However, it would become my job to bring him up to speed (train him) on who the customers were, what their particular preferences and pet peeves were, and, foremost, what their expectations were. It was like rubbing salt in my all-too-fresh wound.

The training process continued after my former boss's departure. The new guy wasn't quite ready or able to assume all of his new responsibilities, but according to management, he was *the candidate with significantly more experience*. Why, then, was I doing his job? It didn't help that he began to receive kudos for his good work—my work. How could management have been so blind as not to see that I was a superior choice? The thoughts of discrimination kept coming back to mind. I was training my boss, he was getting the recognition for my work, and management had covered its eyes with the proverbial blinders. I was more disappointed than ever.

After months of this farce, the frustration and anger I felt had risen to a boiling point, and I knew I had to make a change. Ditching my job of five years was not an immediate option, but I told myself that there had to be something better than what I was currently faced with.

ASKING FOR GUIDANCE

Having realized that this was no longer the right job for me, I sought guidance to receive wisdom regarding the path I should take.

As with any decision, I started with prayer. I asked God for direction and help in seeing what I was to do next. I needed to understand what lesson he was trying to teach me. This meant I had to wait for God to show me the way—PATIENCE.

Patience wasn't necessarily one of my strongest characteristics, but while I waited, I sought advice and encouragement from Greg, my husband, my partner, and my trusted advisor. I knew he would be a voice of reason and could suggest a viable solution for me—and he did.

The first thing out of Greg's mouth was "Just get another job!" That was the response I had already heard from many of my friends and colleagues, and they were all correct. I *could* just get another job somewhere else where my skills and knowledge would be challenged and appreciated. But for some reason, I knew in my gut that that wasn't the answer—though I didn't know yet what the right answer was. So I stayed put and didn't rush to a decision.

MY CORPORATE ASPIRATIONS

"Get a good-paying job" was just what my late father had instructed me to do from a young age. Born and raised in Birmingham, Alabama, the youngest of five children to Junior Dale Bridges, a man far wiser than the sixth-grade education he possessed, and Alma Bridges, a retired domestic and nurse's assistant, my father had mandated that I get a good education, a good job, and marry a great man—in that order. I took those words to heart.

I earned a BS in finance from the University of Alabama at Birmingham one day after marrying my soul mate, R. Gregory Freeland, a presidential management intern whom I had met while spending the previous summer in Maryland with my sister, Gwen. She had introduced us with the hopes of providing me with someone my own age to hang out with during my visit, never imagining that we would begin dating and ultimately marry. To this day, she still says that she had nothing to do with it and that it definitely wasn't her intent, although she adored Greg.

While my father was wary of my dating Greg during my senior year of college, albeit long distance, he was not taking the chance of me becoming distracted and of my studies suffering while I was so close to graduation. As graduation neared, my father warmed to Greg and accepted him as a positive influence in my life. He was satisfied that I would indeed earn that valuable degree. My mother, on the other hand, was a Greg supporter from day one. Unbeknown to my father, or so I thought, she even helped Greg and me stay in touch long distance between Birmingham and Maryland that year.

What neither of them knew at first was that I had accepted Greg's marriage proposal back in September of 1984, just two months after our initial meeting. I knew instinctively that he was the one for me, and it didn't matter whether we had known each other for two months or two years. This time, I trusted my gut.

Although I am typically very conservative in my decision making, needing first to get all the facts and weigh all my options, this willingness to go with my gut on a major life decision set an important precedent for me. Still, Greg and I kept the engagement quiet until February of 1985. As graduation finally approached, I knew my father would be more accepting of the idea.

We were married on June 1, 1985, and I graduated from the University of Alabama on June 2. On June 5, I left Alabama and moved to Maryland to build a life with my new husband. Greg would say he "rescued me from the cotton fields of Alabama," even though I have never picked cotton a day in my life. Although I didn't exactly follow my father's orders regarding education, job, and then marriage, I was only one day off, and he was proud of my accomplishments and pleased with my decisions.

With Greg's help with my résumé, albeit limited, and his network of associates and friends, within 30 days of my arrival to Maryland I landed my first job, with a government contractor in Rockville. Although it wasn't the Wall Street job I had dreamed of, my new degree and irrelevant work experience were apparently enough to get me hired. It would be there that I would learn about the federal government appropriations and procurement process, which would serve me well later in my career. I changed jobs twice before settling in as program analyst at my last employer and returning to school part-time to pursue an MBA from the University of Maryland at College Park. Within two years, I had earned an advanced degree, but in the end, it wouldn't be enough to earn me the promotion I deserved.

A NEW PATH APPEARS

By this point, several months later, Greg and I had fallen into a routine with respect to my employment situation. I would come home from work, and over dinner, we would discuss the disappointment, resentment, and frustration I felt in my current job. Greg was completely supportive and tried to be helpful, but after hearing me complain repeatedly about the same situation, his patience was running thin.

One evening, when "the discussion" began yet again, he asked me, "So what are you going to *do* about it?"

"The only thing I *can* do is get another job and start over," I told him yet again. "But that doesn't seem like it would be an improvement."

"Then if that's not an improvement or won't make you happy, start your own business," he said, almost exasperated.

"I know nothing about starting a business," I said, shaking my head. But even as I spoke, something inside me told me that this idea needed to be explored. I had never considered becoming an entrepreneur—I didn't know any entrepreneurs, knew nothing about the process of starting a company, and had never aspired to become a business owner. However, this was the first alternative that had emerged that didn't involve me working for my current employer or a new one.

Intrigued, I began researching the idea by spending hours and hours at the library and scouring everything I could get my hands on about starting a business. My natural reaction to any new situation or quandary is to gather as much information on it as I can in order to make an informed decision. This situation was no different. I threw myself into studying entrepreneurship like it was my job—and it was, in a way, or I needed to find out whether it *could* be my job.

I find it ironic that when I want to move quickly, the answer comes slowly. I did not believe that God planned for me to stay in my current position, where I was unappreciated, but so far he had not yet pointed me in a new direction. As discouraged as I was, I didn't want to make a hasty decision in anger, such as quitting my job without a backup plan. I looked for a sign, some indication from God that I was on the right path.

While I waited for confirmation that owning my own company was indeed the step I was to take, the idea of becoming an entrepreneur began to resonate with me. The more I thought about it, the more it excited me. But I was still waiting for God's confirmation, so I didn't want to rush ahead. However, holding myself back was becoming more difficult.

My Plan B (The Backup Plan)

I continued to head to work every morning, but my heart wasn't in it. Yes, it was a paycheck, but I no longer felt any allegiance to my employer. Don't get me wrong; I did my work, and I did it well. But my days were drudgery. After work was a different story, however. At night, I now had a new mission, devising a backup plan (my plan B): starting a new company.

At the outset, I had no idea what kind of business I would ultimately start, but I proceeded to fill out and file the paperwork to form Freeland and Associates, a sole proprietorship. In doing so, I felt a glimmer of hope that I was headed in the right direction. Evaluating my new business concept while working a full-time job fulfilled my dual needs of paying our bills on time and pursuing a potential new career—entrepreneur.

No one at work was aware, or needed to be aware, of my career and business planning.

My first step, which should be the first step of any business plan, was to determine what products or services I would offer customers. Because my background was in services, I opted to explore opportunities there first, by looking at my background and existing skill set. These included the following:

- Finance
- Program management
- Federal government contracting
- Human resource management
- Customer service

As I studied what I had done career-wise, I realized that my government contracting experience was what differentiated me. It was also the one industry with which I was most familiar.

Next, I had to assess whether there was a viable market for such a service offering. Were customers willing to pay me for my work? And would they be willing to pay enough to make the business successful? Those were key questions to which I needed to find answers.

Fortunately, starting in the early 1990s, the federal government began committing an enormous amount of resources to information technology (IT) initiatives, such as consolidation and networking of IT systems, upgrades from legacy systems to Web-based systems, software development, and more. It was also a time when small businesses were dominating the industry with high-tech innovations. Opportunities were seemingly plentiful for those familiar with this marketplace, as I was.

Although my personal background was not in IT, the more I researched, the more I became convinced that program management coupled with IT solutions could be a powerful service offering for Freeland and Associates. However, I needed the right strategy and the right people at the right time to make it work.

BIRTHING A SON AND A COMPANY

I progressed with my study of the federal contracting market by night and with work at my employer by day, and in the spring of 1991, I learned that I was pregnant with our first child. It was at the same time scary and exciting, much like starting a company.

Just as I was preparing to embark on my entrepreneurial venture, Greg and I prepared ourselves for an important addition to our family. We were eager to meet our child and happy about expanding our family. I went to the doctor for routine exams in between work, research, and business planning, consistently getting a thumbs-up from him on my weight gain and the baby. Things were progressing smoothly, or so I thought.

That sense of peace was shattered on December 11, 1991, when, on the day before my twenty-ninth birthday, my water broke six weeks before my scheduled delivery date. I immediately sensed that something was wrong—it was too soon for the baby to come—but as Greg and I drove to the hospital, only a short distance from our home in Clinton, Maryland, I tried to reassure myself that all would be fine.

Once we arrived at the emergency room and I got hooked up to the sonogram machine, the look on the face of the attending physician showed that he was concerned. There was a problem with the baby that the hospital could not handle, so I was transported by ambulance—sirens blaring the whole way—with Greg and my sister, Gwen, to Georgetown University Hospital in Washington, D.C. It was the longest ride of my life. With each passing mile, the baby inched closer and closer to being born.

Within minutes after I arrived in the labor and delivery room, our baby was born. He was a beautiful 3-lb., 10-oz. boy, whom we named Richard Gregory Freeland II, after his father.

The reason for the rush to Georgetown was that this precious little boy was born with an object the size of an orange located on the outside of his stomach, called an omphalocele. The doctors explained that this was a birth defect in which part of the intestine protrudes outside the abdomen. It can be repaired by surgery, which the hospital had performed on other babies, but because of Gregory's size and the size of the omphalocele, surgery was not an immediate option. The only thing that could be done at that time was to apply pressure and try to slowly squeeze it back into place under his lungs, where it belonged. All we could do was pray and wait and wonder why this problem had not been detected by my obstetricians in utero. However, at that moment, we couldn't worry too much about the incompetence of my medical team; we would deal with that later. In the meantime, we prayed for God's healing upon this precious child.

We started prayer chains and prayer circles and contacted prayer warriors around the world to pray for our baby. We knew that he needed divine intervention to survive, but we needed those prayers to sustain us as well. A few days later, we received a glimmer of hope: the baby finally opened his eyes and looked into mine. His expression told me that everything was OK. From then on, I rarely left his bedside. I was there day in, day out, praying, crying, and longing for a miracle.

Christmas 1991 came and went and, soon after, New Year's Day 1992. With each passing day, our faith that he would survive strengthened. However, in mid-January we received devastating news. The orange-sized membrane was not shrinking back into the cavity where it belonged, and now the baby's organs were being affected. The baby we had begun calling "Little Greg" was in a critical state. He was still too small and the membrane too large to risk an operation, so we could only wait and pray again for a miracle. Wait was really all that we could do—but there had to be something more. We were at one of the leading hospitals in the area; surely they could do something more.

With doctors telling us they could do nothing else, we called our pastor, Grainger Browning III of Ebenezer African Methodist Episcopal Church in Fort Washington, Maryland. He came and prayed and anointed Little Greg, reassuring us that God was still able to heal him and that God was in control. We had to pray, keep hope, and exercise our faith now more than ever. This was a true test of faith, love, and courage, a test we had not faced before.

On January 30, 1992, his fiftieth day of life, Little Greg opened his eyes and looked at me, and although I couldn't hold him in my arms,

I looked deep into his eyes to let him know that we loved him. At the same time, my heart ached and was slowly breaking with each passing moment. Later that day, his uncle, Reverend Calvin Freeland, came to baptize him. The nurses in the neonatal intensive care unit (NICU) dressed him in a white baptismal gown and hat and laid him on his bed. He looked like an angel. The baptism was our way of committing him back to God, not knowing how long he would be with us. We were sure that the Lord was watching over us all.

His breathing was shallow but steady, so the nurses urged me to go home, get some rest, and come back later. I hesitated but then agreed. As we walked into our house, the phone was ringing, and I knew at that moment that he was gone. During the 20-mile drive home, Little Greg had passed away. He was now with God.

The trek back to Georgetown was the longest and emptiest drive I had ever taken. At the end of the trip would be my one and only opportunity to hold my son, still wrapped in his white baptismal gown. My heart was broken. Everyone in the room was in tears. Even now as I write this, the tears flow freely. The stillness and peacefulness of his body reassured me that he now rested with the Father in heaven. I also knew that we would forever have a guardian angel looking down on us from heaven. Although only 50 days young, he touched many in his life, and that is why my son was such a special child.

Inspiring a Company

During the time that Gregory was physically with us, I didn't once think about work or my company to-be. While it had been my focus during the months before my son's life and death, it had ceased to be important during the special time he was with us.

Once Little Greg was gone, Greg and I took some time away to plan a life without our son. It was gut-wrenching, but we knew we had to find a way to honor him and begin our lives again. We needed time to mourn the tragic loss of our son. We knew that we would never get over it, but we had to find a way to move ahead.

After returning to work, I realized that I was also mourning the loss of the job that I expected would be mine. Together, both losses made me more determined than ever to make my company a reality. At that moment, Freeland and Associates ceased to exist, and RGII Technologies was birthed—named after my now deceased son, **R**ichard **G**regory **II**.

ENTREPRENEURIAL SELF-ASSESSMENT

To help you decide what your business might look like and what products or services you could specialize in, answer the following questions.

1. What kind of training do you have?
2. Which of your skills are you most proud of or confident in?
3. What kinds of work, school, or volunteer experiences do you have that could be business related?
4. What hobbies or interests do you have?
5. What particular industries or markets have you worked within?
6. Are there companies you admire? Which ones?
7. Are there particular types of businesses that interest you more than others: retail, wholesale, manufacturing, service, online, etc.?

Now read back through your responses for inspiration and ideas regarding businesses about which you could become passionate. Merely being interested in a business is not enough; you need to be able to throw yourself into it 110%. If you don't feel strongly enough yet, you may not be ready to take the entrepreneurial leap.

LESSONS LEARNED

Make knowing your propensity for risk a key component of the entrepreneurial decision making process.

☑ Your desire to start your own company may emerge from frustration or dissatisfaction with your employer, as it did for me, but do not let those reasons be your driving force. Being excited by the prospect of controlling your own destiny is more important than trying to prove something to someone else.

☑ Entrepreneurs often take risk in order to succeed, starting with forming the business, but they are not inherent risk takers. They do not go looking for long shots.

☑ Do not rush your decision making. Ask for guidance from your higher power and from people who know you well before you take the leap. Make sure it is the path you were meant to take.

☑ Evaluate your background, interests, skills, and experience to find the type of business that will fit you long-term. Ideally, you will discover a venture that blends your interests and abilities in a high-growth market.

☑ Just because you are well suited to start a particular type of business does not mean that it is a viable or potentially successful company. Research your market to identify how large it is, who your competition is, and whether you can be profitable at the outset with a very small percentage of the market.

☑ If you decide that your business concept is not viable, look for ways to tweak your market focus, approach, service/product offering, niche, or some other aspect of the business before moving to the next step, business planning.

CHAPTER 2

PLANNING
FOR THE JOURNEY

*"...for the vision is yet for an appointed time, but at the end it
shall speak and not lie: though it tarry, wait for it;
because it will surely come, it will not tarry." — Habakkuk 2:3*

Having determined where I needed to head career-wise, my next step was to begin planning how to get there. Without any experience in starting a company or any role models or experienced colleagues, I faced an uphill battle in figuring out how to get from where I was to where I wanted to be.

I wasn't yet ready to make a break from my employer, despite the unfair treatment—like everyone else, we had bills to pay—so I continued to work full-time. However, during evenings and weekends, my focus was devoted almost exclusively to my new business, which had become my driving force.

Given that I had no knowledge of what it took to be an entrepreneur, had no capital to invest and no network of investors to draw from, and had always thought of myself as risk averse, I recognized that achieving success as an entrepreneur would be a major challenge for me. Yet, with my husband's confidence in me and my faith that I was on the path that the Lord wanted me on, I moved ahead, determined to give it my best shot.

That First Step

After months of working on my business plan, the time had come to put up or shut up. I needed feedback from actual potential customers to gauge whether I had any chance of succeeding in a venture of this magnitude. I felt in my bones that the proposition could be viable but knew that I couldn't be objective at that point.

So I approached one of my employer's former customers, someone with whom I had worked closely at one point but who was no longer affiliated with my employer. We had stayed in contact, and, first and foremost, I wanted to get his assessment of my business proposition. But I had other intentions as well: I also wanted to ask him to consider my no-experience company for a small-task order contract—in other words, take a chance on me to perform a task that could be funded via a purchase-order-type contract for under $25,000. This would be a bold request from me, but I knew that bold ideas required bold steps, and this was just one of the many bodacious moves that I would make on my journey.

After paying him several visits, I was finally able to convince him that I had not only a plan but also the necessary skills to get the job done. He needed someone to perform a cost impact analysis on what it would take to overhaul his department's information technology infrastructure. Personally, I knew absolutely nothing about what he was trying to do—and I told him that up front—but I knew exactly where to find the right resources to get the project done for him, on time and within the allotted budget.

To prepare the relatively small proposal, I tapped my network of contacts and found just the right IT professional to do the work. He was knowledgeable about IT infrastructures, systems, networking, and applications and could decipher what the task at hand would entail. With his skill set, we were able to prepare a solid proposal that convincingly demonstrated to the client a future state of the department's infrastructure. We prepared the bid and won the contract for the $25,000 project, which was with the Department of the Navy. It wasn't a lot of money, but that didn't matter as much as the fact that I now had a customer. I was building a track record and a legitimate customer base.

Because my goal was to do business with the federal government, that first contract was critical. I learned early on that small businesses have to be able to show prospective clients that they have won and successfully performed on a contract for other government agencies. This is what constitutes "past performance," one of the key factors in determining whether a company will be properly positioned for future opportunities to bid on other government contracts. We were on our way, and the journey was about to begin.

THE 8(A) ADVANTAGE

From my years of business experience working with government contractors, I knew that the federal government was a lucrative market. It had sustained several of my former employers, as well as my current one, and I was convinced that it could sustain RGII Technologies once I gained access.

In my efforts to finish my business plan, I turned to the Small Business Administration (SBA), which then referred me to the Service Corps of Retired Executives (SCORE) (www.score.org), an SBA-sponsored organization of experienced business owners. The members volunteer their time to help new companies get started and assist business owners in overcoming obstacles they encounter along the way. My meeting with SCORE was a turning point in my business. During my experience there, I first heard of the 8(a) Business Development Program, a program named for a section of the Small Business Act passed in 1953 to establish the SBA. The act was designed to "encourage" and "develop" small-business growth and to aid minorities and other disadvantaged people in securing loans and learning management techniques. Although the act favors the disadvantaged, assistance is not limited to members based on race (see U.S. Library of Congress at http://thomas. loc.gov). This program eventually catapulted me into entrepreneurship as a lifelong career.

For those unfamiliar with the 8(a) Business Development Program, it was established to assist eligible small, disadvantaged businesses in competing in the American economy through business development. (Source: 13 CFR 124.1 - Code of Federal Regulations Section 13.124.1). Furthermore, the program allows for qualified minority and disadvantaged participants to pursue and compete for government contracts that are set aside specifically for companies with the 8(a) designation, as certified by the SBA. Each fiscal year, October 1 through September 30, the U.S. government sets annual targets for the percent of contracts each government agency will award to 8(a) businesses. Participants in the 8(a) program have a unique advantage in that they are given training on how to identify the appropriate buyers in each agency and which agency is buying the products or services they are selling. However, applying for and gaining admission to the 8(a) program does not guarantee that a company will ultimately win any government contracts. 8(a) is a self-marketing program, so it is only as good as the company's individual marketing and business development strategies. Successful strategies and a continuous pavement-pounding mentality give small businesses an oftentimes coveted entrée into the government market—but no more. From there, selling the company and its myriad services and know-how is now up to the business owner.

The 8(a) program is a nine-year program divided into two stages: developmental, four years in duration, and transitional, the remaining five years. Certified participants gain access to a plethora of available resources, ranging from business planning and mentoring to procurement assistance, business counseling, financial assistance, management training, and other business services. The goal is to help 8(a) companies gain access to the broad government contract market-place, develop industry-specific work experience, and then ultimately transfer the government-learned experience to the full and open commercial markets. The objective at the end of the nine-year program, affectionately referred to as "graduation," is for the company to be entirely self-sufficient, remain viable, and compete without the set-asides and the perceived shelter of the program.

In researching the 8(a) program, I saw that companies of all sizes were participating, including micro, small, midsized, and larger companies. That was encouraging. Most participants were using the program as intended, as a tool or a launching pad into the federal market that could lead to larger, more lucrative government contracts. What I learned gave me hope that with the right strategy and team, I too could do well in this market. I also recognized that the viability of my company hinged on my ability to first get accepted into the program and then use 8(a) as a stepping-stone and not a crutch.

Some of the tools the SBA gave me as part of my study of the 8(a) program included reports on current participants, companies in my area, companies that offered services similar to mine who were doing business with certain agencies, as well as the reported size of each company. I was encouraged when I saw the number of local companies having success as part of the program. I grew more confident that I could do it, that I could become an entrepreneur, and the 8(a) program could be the catalyst. The only thing standing in the way of my success was applying and being accepted as an 8(a) participant. However, the company had to meet a few eligibility requirements before submitting the application.

First, the company had to be owned and controlled by a person who was both socially and economically disadvantaged. That requirement was met hands down. I was African American, a presumed qualifying group under the Small Business Act, and my net worth was significantly below the $250,000 to meet the economically disadvantaged test. Second, the company had to meet a small-business size standard.

The size standard is a numerical standard based on the number of employees or annual sales/receipts of the business. With one employee (me) and a $25,000 purchase order contract, I would also meet the size standard requirement. Third, I had to be able to show that the business had a reasonable chance of success. I would have to prove this based solely on my personal background and experience, my MBA degree, my government purchase order, a solid customer endorsement, a detailed market analysis, and a strong business plan, which was a work in progress. Fourth, I had to display good/strong character. I wondered how to do that on a written application. The answer was clear: tell the truth about who you are as a person, your beliefs, and why you believe you deserve this opportunity. I also included personal references from those who could attest to my character. A good credit score, indicating a track record of paying obligations on time, was an added bonus. The last and final hurdle was the one I found to be the hardest: the company had to have been in business for two years. At the time of application on November 22, 1993, I had technically been in business for two years. I say "technically" because I was still working full-time and still conducting, albeit off and on, the study, one iteration after another, supported by a few small, incremental funding adjustments to the purchase order. It was enough to meet the application requirements but no guarantee of acceptance. The application would take months to complete and turned out to be 22 pages long. All I could do was pray for acceptance. Because only a fraction of applicants were approved, this would be no small feat.

STEP ONE IN THE JOURNEY

The bad news about the 8(a) application is that it is comprehensive. The good news about the 8(a) application is that it is comprehensive. That is, the application leads you through all of the major questions that you will need to address in a formal business plan. Once you have completed your application, you are well on your way to a solid plan you can use to pursue financing for your company. Instructions for the 8(a) application include registering at Central Contractor Registration (CCR) and registering for an account at the SBA's General Log-in-System (GLS) in order for the SBA to communicate with you about your application. This information can be found at https://sba8a.symplicity.com/applicants/guide.

Keep in mind that in 1993, this online resource was not available; everything was done manually, by hand, and submitted through the snail-mail system. Even then, SBA had a 90-day processing time for all applications received—and that's really swift for the highly bureaucratic federal government. Completing the application step by step, I was forced to think through my target market, potential clients, hiring needs, financing sources, and revenue projections, among other key business decisions. I was also proactive and attended workshops and seminars in my area about business planning, to give myself the best chance for success. Of course, this was done on my days off or while on "slick" leave. Many of these workshops were sponsored by either SBA or the county's economic development office and the local chamber of commerce.

Despite the fact that I had business experience, an MBA, and familiarity with my industry, I had no training in writing a business plan. It was daunting! "Overwhelming" is probably the best word to describe it. This is where many entrepreneurs get stuck; they get overwhelmed with the process and can't figure out how to move forward. A large percent give up on their dream of owning their own business because they hit a roadblock, their business plan.

Although I was unnerved by how much information I needed to gather and think through, I attacked the plan little by little, one piece at a time, taking time to do research when I encountered a question that I didn't know how to answer. Research in the early '90s didn't entail the multitude of Internet sites that are available today on how to write a business plan. Sites such as www.freebusinessplans.com did not exist. My research included trips to the library and visits to meet with SCORE consultants.

While the 8(a) application is no substitute for a business plan, key sections in the application would ultimately help me formulate the plan. Remember that the business plan is the road map to a viable, successful business. Now, I know that some entrepreneurs minimize the importance of a business plan, especially when struggling to survive. However, the time spent on this fluid document, in my opinion, is critical at every phase of the company, especially during start up. One must remember that specific sections should be included in every business plan; you need to carefully think through and describe each in a detailed written document. Daunting yes, necessary absolutely, doable without question. You can do it; it just takes time.

Our Business Plan Outline

Granted, every business plan is different, but such plans need to follow a standard outline in order to be truly complete. Yes, you can modify this outline somewhat if you prefer, but make sure that you still address each of the sections I've listed. Don't leave any out. For example, feel free to move the "Management Team" section elsewhere, but you can't delete it and still have a solid plan. The same goes for the other sections; you can rename them or put them in a different spot within the plan document, but don't delete them.

Also keep in mind that nearly all successful businesses have a business plan to guide their growth, whether they needed funding to get off the ground or not. A business plan helps you get from where you are to where you want to be, money aside. The process of thinking through what you need to do to reach your goals is invaluable.

Your completed plan should be approximately 40–50 pages long—not 200, not 10, but long enough to provide the detail that bankers and investors expect without overloading them with unnecessary details.

Executive summary. Your executive summary is a two- to three-page synopsis of your entire plan. It hits the high points of the package, giving readers an idea of what kind of business you're in and what strategies you'll use to be successful. Many venture capitalists read only the executive summary because they are inundated with so many plans that they could not possibly read them all. For that reason, your executive summary may be the only section of the plan that is read, so you need to make darn sure it's superb.

Many business owners write this section last, once all of the other pieces are in place and they are better able to address questions surrounding the who, what, when, where, why, and how of their new company.

Business environment. This section of the business plan helps educate the reader regarding the marketplace in which you are operating, whether it is the federal government, the retail market, health care, financial services, tool and die, food service, you name it. In what industry/market will you be doing business? For instance, the business environment section of our plan stated "RGII Technologies is headquartered in Annapolis, Maryland, a 30–35-minute commute from the Washington, D.C., metropolitan area. D.C. is the headquarters for the majority of federal government departments and agencies and therefore provides for a substantial business base. With the national economy taking a turn for the better, the opportunities for attaining the company's short- and long-term objectives will be optimized." Can you tell this was written by a novice? Indeed, it was what I understood the business environment to be at the time. Today, more learned, I would write it slightly differently. Some facts remain the same, such as federal government departments still providing for a substantial business base. However, some things are quite different. At the time of this writing, the national economy is taking a turn for the worse, toward a recession.

Identifying your industry or market should be relatively easy. Next, a good business plan will provide relevant background on what you, as the business owner, deem to be the success factors for thriving in the business environment. In other words, what does it take to succeed in your industry?

Some key facts and figures you'll want to research include the following.

- *Industry size.* What is the total value of all the revenue being earned in this market? Is it $4 million? $400 million? $4 billion?
- *Competitors.* Who are the players (both small fish and large fish) in the marketplace pond, and how much market share do they possess? How will you be able to compete and win as a very small fish? What are your discriminators? What makes you so different from all the rest?
- *Industry growth rate.* How quickly is the industry growing for companies your size?
- *High-growth niches.* Have you identified pockets of opportunity that are growing faster than average?
- *Trends.* What market trends are shaping opportunities for you and other participants? Will new legislation help or hinder your ability to penetrate the market?
- *Technology.* What technological shifts or innovations are shaping the direction of the industry and coming opportunities?
- *Legislation.* What recent or pending legislation is impacting how current and future players do business? What threats or opportunities have emerged that will help or possibly hinder your ability to penetrate the market? How will you mitigate any foreseen or unforeseen risks?
- *Customers.* Who are the typical customers for your product or service? Are they governments (federal, state, or local), the

average consumer, other businesses, wholesalers, nonprofits?
Know thy customer.

- *Marketing approach.* What key message or strategy has proven
  to work in this space? What are the triggers that spark interest
  from potential customers? Is it a track record of superior performance, the ability to deliver quality and added value, operating
  with honesty and integrity, offering competitive costs, providing
  new innovations, etc.?

Comprehensively researching these areas will help focus your plan
and identify the make-or-break facets of the business environment in
which you will operate. If your product or service is consumer driven
and you are targeting a particular geographic area, you will find the
state's statistical abstract to be of help in describing the population base,
corporate headquarters, growth rate, and local issues contributing to
or hampering business growth in the region. For statistical information on how companies that do business with the federal government
have fared, one reliable source is the Federal Procurement Data System
(FPDS), on the Web at www.fpds.gov.

Business description. Your business description, or business history,
section consists first of facts: when and how the business started, who
makes up the management team, what the legal structure of the business
is, what the company's product or service line of business is, who its
customer base is. Second, it is of an aspirational nature, about the future
of the business and where it is headed.

When and how the business was started will be unique to each business owner. For me, it was in the basement of my house in the early
'90s as a result of what I termed discrimination in the workplace. This
description is tailored to each individual's personal start-up story. The
description of the management team in this section is brief because a
full section is committed to the management team later. However, a brief
look at who owns the company and their background and employment
history, along with work experience and backgrounds of the remaining

key management members, may be included here. Again, this section later in the plan is crucial to letting the readers know with whom they will be working.

The legal structure of the business will have to be determined on the basis of who will own the company and the owner's business objectives, keeping in mind the following different types of structures.

- *Sole proprietorship.* The oldest, most common, and simplest form of business organization, owned and managed by one person.
- *Close corporation.* A corporation permitted by state law to operate more informally than most corporations (allowing decisions without meetings of the board of directors) and that has only a limited number of shareholders.
- *S corporation.* A corporation that makes a valid election to be taxed under Subchapter S of Chapter 1 of the Internal Revenue Code. S Corporations generally do not pay any income taxes; instead, the corporation's income or losses are divided among and passed on to its shareholders.
- *C corporation.* A corporation that may have an unlimited number of shareholders and whose income is taxed under 26 U.S.C. § 11 and Subchapter C of the Internal Revenue Code.
- *Limited liability company (LLC).* A business structure that offers limited liability to its owners. It is somewhat of a hybrid, having the characteristics of a corporation and a partnership.
- *Limited liability partnership (LLP).* A business structure where all partners have a form of limited liability for each individual's protection within the partnership and the partners have the right to manage the business directly.

The list above is not intended to be all inclusive. The above information, along with additional information, can be found at www.irs.gov or www.sba.gov. Research each type of structure in detail, and work closely with a legal professional to help in identifying the right structure for you. As indicated earlier, my company started out as a sole proprietorship; however, as the business dynamics changed, so did the legal structure. Each legal structure decision was based purely on the evolution and growth of the company—but I maintained 100% ownership from beginning to end.

The company's product or service line and its customer base provide the reader with insight into what you are selling and to whom. Although this too will be covered in a section of its own later, a brief description here would be appropriate. For instance, our initial product line was computer services and management consulting provided to the federal government. Doesn't say a whole lot, does it? As the company matured, the service line would read "provide information technology services and solutions to federal government agencies, including the Departments of Commerce, Transportation, and Labor."

With the factual information included in the business description, the reader will have a better understanding of how your business came to be and what value it offers the customer.

The second part is less fact and more hopeful—keeping in mind that hope is not a strategy (see *Hope Is Not a Strategy* by Rick Page). In other words, this part of the plan is the owner's projections or "pie in the sky" leader's vision for the company. Here you would describe where you project the company to be five years from now. What is the projected revenue and employee count? Who are the major customers? What about market share, growth rate, profitability, return on investment, etc.? How will you achieve these projections, how will you fund the growth, and what funding sources do you currently have available? All of these questions should be answered here. Do not leave anything to the imagination of the reader or cause the reader to second-guess the plan. You must be convincing and confident while giving a big-picture perspective of where the business is headed.

With all of the above information included, the business description section is only one to two pages long, enough to highlight the who, what, when, and how of the company.

Product or service description. After describing the business entity, in this section you will describe the types of products or services you'll sell to your target market. You will want to list each of your offerings—in our case, IT services—as well as their features and benefits.

For example, our company started as a computer services and management consulting firm, a relatively generic line of business, but evolved into information technology services and solutions. The one important thing to remember is that regardless of how small or large your product or service offering might be, you should briefly describe what it entails and the value-added benefit it brings to the customer. For instance, under IT services and solutions, I would include a brief description of our capability in the areas of requirements analysis, network design and engineering, systems engineering/integration, help desk support, database/application development, and so on. The benefit to the customer would include cost efficiencies, downtime minimization, system uptime maximization, increased productivity, etc. Here you sell the company and its value proposition.

This section will run one to four pages, depending on the complexity of your product or service. High-tech and revolutionary offerings, as in my case, may require several pages in order to adequately explain the technology and its benefits to the customer.

Competition. "Know thy competition" is what I always say. Figuring out who the competitors are will take some research and digging. If you operate locally and in consumer-based products or services, the Yellow Page listings are a decent starting point. With the massive federal government being my market and the customers not being everyday consumers, the Yellow Pages would prove ineffective. I turned to the SBA, the very agency responsible for assisting small businesses, to help gather the information on the competition. From SBA I obtained summary listings on the small, women-owned, and 8(a) companies currently doing business with the government. This list was massive, so I had to narrow it to those companies located within 50–100 miles of my geographic location. The Small Business Advocates within government agencies, along with the central contract registry (www.ccr.gov), are another excellent resource if you intend to target the government market. Sources outside of the government market that are helpful include your local economic development department and chamber of commerce, the Thomas Register (www.thomasnet.com) for industrial companies, Dun and Bradstreet (www.dnb.com), trade journals, local media/publications, and the Internet. The Internet was not available during my start-up days but is an invaluable research tool today.

Simply having the names of your competitors isn't enough. You also need to know, among other things:

- Who the major players are in your industry or market
- What percent of your total market they control, i.e., market share
- How large they are, revenue-wise and employee-wise (this information is often proprietary and not easily obtained)
- What their geographic service area is and how it overlaps with yours
- Who their largest customers are
- What their strengths and weaknesses are
- What their biggest hindrances/threats to continued growth are
- Where their biggest opportunities lie

With that information, you can then highlight your company's competitive advantages as well as elaborate on how you will exploit your competitors' weaknesses. Keep in mind that you too have business weaknesses. Your ability to clarify your plan of action to rectify your business weaknesses will help to mitigate the risk associated with your business plan.

Management team. As stated in the business description above, the management team section is one of the most critical sections of your business plan, especially if you plan to be more than a one-woman/man show or will be pursuing any form of financing. The description of your management team can make or break the business. Banks want to know whom they are dealing with and who will be responsible (whose head is on the line, so to speak) when considering lending your company money. The depth and breadth of experience possessed by your management team yield better odds of obtaining funding. In the beginning, that person was me, and everything was riding on my abilities and background. Therefore, I moved this section to the front of the plan. In the case where you have a senior executive team already in place and its affiliation with your company becomes a discriminating factor or is listed as a competitive advantage, I recommend moving this section to the front of the business plan. It should be one of the first sections lenders read so that you immediately capture their attention and highlight the level of expertise and skills involved in the company.

Within this section you need to do the following:

- Identify each management team member by name
- Detail members' past experiences and backgrounds, emphasizing the talents you intend to leverage
- Discuss their roles within your business, including job responsibilities

Hit hard on past experiences and successes as much as possible in this section. I learned very early on that the employees and their skill sets are a company's greatest assets. Detailing the expertise, experience, and value that key employees contribute to the company is paramount.

Organizational structure. In addition to defining the roles your key executives will fill, developing a hiring plan is also important. What kind of workers will you need during the next few months? What positions will they hold? When will you hire them? How much will you pay them? What will their primary responsibilities be? Which department will they join? Which customer will they support?

One of the easiest ways to explain your company's future organizational structure is to create an organizational chart. Draw solid rectangles to indicate current positions and dashed rectangles to indicate positions to be filled in the future. In the beginning, my organizational chart had one solid rectangle and multiple dashed boxes, similar to the chart below:

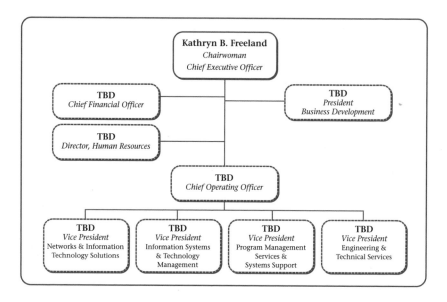

In the beginning, it was just me, and I hadn't hired anyone at that point. Therefore, all the proposed positions would read "TBD," to be determined.

Many companies set milestones that need to be reached before particular positions will be filled. These could be revenue targets, new customers, or specific contracts. Balancing your need for more help with your cash flow is tricky, but an organizational chart will show the reader the organizational structure you envision and the type of people you will need to help execute your vision.

Marketing plan. After describing the inner workings of your new venture, explain the strategies you will use to pursue new business. Your marketing plan should clearly identify and describe your target markets as well as the marketing methods you will use to communicate with them. Some of the most effective marketing tools that small businesses use include the following:

- Web site: no widespread usage in early 1990s but a "must-have" today
- Collateral materials: brochures, capabilities statements, company highlights (one pager)
- Business cards
- Stationery
- Public relations
- Networking: offline and online
- Advertising: print, broadcast, outdoor, pay-per-click
- Newsletter: offline or online
- Face-to-face meetings
- Tradeshow booths

The general guideline for how much you should spend on marketing ranges from 4% to 10%, with newer companies spending closer to 10% of their gross sales.

Your plan should list all of the methods you intend to use, how much you have set aside for each initiative, and a schedule of when activities will occur. It can be as elaborate or simple as you want it to be, as long as you have the resources to pay for it.

Financial plan. The financial projections were the hardest for us to pull together because we were trying to be realistic but still demonstrate that we could think big. Preparing cash flow projections, a balance sheet, and a profit and loss statement for the coming year was hard enough, but having to realistically estimate how much business we would be doing in *three* years? That was a long shot "best guesstimate."

Fortunately, we had been making a little money before we submitted our 8(a) application and began working on our business plan, so we weren't starting from square one. We also had a CPA do our taxes to increase the credibility of our numbers. Greg and I did all the number crunching and projections, based on what we perceived our probability of winning each contract would be, and our accountant checked them over for accuracy. Our potential revenue pipeline, as it's referred to, consisted of our best estimate of the chance of winning each contract we identified and were preparing to submit a bid for times the total projected contract value, to reach a projected revenue figure. We added those up, and that was our annual revenue budget.

We started the financial section with a narrative description of the company's current financial position, profit trends, strategies we intended to use to obtain additional working capital, employees (me), revenue, and profits, measly as they were. Because we had been relying on credit cards to fund our growth to date (this will be discussed later as well), we also added a discussion of our credit capacity, meaning that we had ample credit available to us—so much so that it would prohibit us from obtaining a small-business loan later on.

After the description of the business's financial status, we inserted the three years of projected cash flow, our profit and loss statements, and the balance sheet that our accountant had approved.

Opportunities. Although we haven't seen other plans include this, we found the "Opportunities" section in our 8(a) application to work so well that we incorporated it into our formal plan. This section describes the business you have identified, qualified as potential targets, and are prepared to pursue with a reasonable probability to win.

In our case, we listed the contract leads we had received, describing what the contract opportunity was, such as "within the next six months, the Department of Defense will issue a contract for computer programming," and the potential value. These were the contracts we were aggressively pursuing as part of our IT service offering. We knew that if we were fortunate to win, we would have to hire IT professionals with the necessary skills to perform the work. I call this a catch-22: "We won," and, oh, by the way, "We won"—now we have to perform.

Appendix. An appendix can be included as a catchall for relevant supporting material that didn't fit elsewhere within the plan, such as executive résumés, contracts, reports, or articles.

We completed the 8(a) application in three or four months, nearly two years after I had officially formed Freeland and Associates and subsequently RGII Technologies. The application was submitted on November 22, 1993, and we received notification that it had been approved on January 24, 1994, just 60 days later. Now the pace of the journey speeds up, and I'm steering the ship to places unknown.

LESSONS LEARNED

Failure to properly plan is a plan destined for failure.

☑ Some of the best resources for help in developing a business plan include the Small Business Administration (SBA), the Service Corps of Retired Executives (SCORE), the Small Business Development Center (SBDC) in your area, and Minority or Women Business Development Centers (MBDCs and WBDCs). Some will assist you in writing your plan, some provide materials to guide you, and others will nearly write it for you, at little or no cost.

☑ The Small Business Administration's 8(a) program is a program designed for economically and socially disadvantaged business owners. It aims to provide a road map for doing business with the federal government. Being accepted into this nine-year program is no easy task, however. After an initial four-year mentoring and training period, companies then spend the subsequent five years fine-tuning their businesses in an effort to successfully compete upon graduation. The knowledge gained while completing the program is transferrable to the highly competitive commercial marketplace.

(continued on page 36)

Lessons Learned

(continued from page 35)

☑ Securing your first customer or client is an important milestone. Convincing someone else to buy from you confirms that you may be on the right track and also gives you the opportunity to start building a past performance track record. Demonstrating that you can fulfill the terms of a contract, that you can successfully complete work to a client's specifications, on-time and within budget, will give potential customers and statekholders, such as bankers, confidence in your vision as a staunch leader and business owner.

☑ A business plan is a critical business tool whether you need outside funding or not. Preparing one forces you to think through how you will build and grow your company, including when you will need to hire your first employee and what skills he or she must have, as well as how you will market the company, what equipment you will need, how you'll beat the competition, and what kind of revenue and expenses you project for the coming three to five years.

☑ Even if you personally prepare your assumptions and financial projections, you would be smart to have a CPA review them for accuracy. If you can add a CPA's statement asserting that the statements have been prepared in accordance with Generally Accepted Accounting Principles (GAAP), you're also ahead of the game in terms of credibility.

☑ Understand that your business plan should mirror your company; it too will grow and change through the years. That means you shouldn't file your plan away and forget about it. Instead, reference it at least quarterly and review where you've been, where you are now, and where you want to be three months hence. Modify your goals and strategies based on where the company is currently, while keeping in mind that the plan is a road map and the map is subject to change.

CHAPTER 3

FUNDING
THE VENTURE

"But my God shall supply all your need according to his riches in glory by Christ Jesus." — Philippians 4:19

The purchase orders from our Navy contract and a new order Greg had secured with the Federal Reserve Board were trickling in, but our sole client didn't yet have the full funding necessary to implement our recommendations. He was pleased with the work we had done on his IT infrastructure study but had little control over his ability to proceed, so we were left waiting for larger contracts to come. The delay in funding slowed our progress toward being full-fledged entrepreneurs. I was certainly ready to leave a company that I felt did not appreciate me, but the purchase order payments weren't enough to cover the business bills and those at home, too.

At this point, Greg was working from home as a consultant and helped out by doing business development and marketing for RGII, including creating a basic capabilities brochure for the company, and by following up on initial government contacts I had made.

Money was getting tighter, but Greg and I felt that it was important to take a much-needed break from the stress of starting a company by getting away to the Bahamas that November. We needed time away, to regroup and to rejuvenate ourselves and our marriage. A few weeks after our return, we discovered that the trip had been fruitful in more ways than one—I was pregnant again.

DOUBLY BLESSED

The pregnancy was considered high risk because of my previous loss and the shape of my uterus. What I learned after Gregory's passing was that I have a septate uterus, meaning that a wall, or septum, divides the uterus into two cavities, which may have significantly limited the baby's ability to grow. With this knowledge, I was especially nervous, but my doctors at Georgetown assured me that the likelihood of a repeat pregnancy like the last was very slim. Still, I went in for regular checkups.

My obstetrician told me that I could maintain my work schedule as long as I was feeling well and getting proper rest, so I continued heading to work every morning and coming home to work on growing RGII. By the time I was four months along, I had slowed down slightly, in part due to my rapidly growing belly, which was unusually large for this stage in my pregnancy.

On a trip to the hospital with my sister for her routine checkup, I began having symptoms that made me anxious, so I found a nurse and was immediately rushed to an examination room for an evaluation. Memories of Little Greg being born raced through my mind, and my fear rose as I waited for my obstetrician, Dr. Jeffrey King. As it turned out, Dr. King was not available, but the doctor on duty immediately ordered a sonogram, followed by a more detailed ultrasound. As the tests continued, my concern for the baby nearly overwhelmed me. Then, I saw a smile on the doctor's face.

The doctor's smile gave me a glimmer of hope that everything was OK.

"Mrs. Freeland, did anyone tell you that you are carrying multiples?" he asked.

"Multiple what?" I asked, confused.

"Multiple babies. As in, more than one," he replied.

I looked at him as if he had horns growing out of his head. What in the world was he talking about? Multiples?

Seeing that I was not yet understanding him, the doctor began circling the number of sacs he saw on the ultrasound image. There were three. However, the symptoms that had prompted the examination indicated that one of the three sacs did not contain a fetus. Yet two of the sacs were intact and doing well. I was having twins!

The news explained my extra weight gain and size, and when I emerged from the examination room and told my sister, she nearly fainted.

I thanked God for protecting the babies and for repaying me double for my trouble: two babies to try to soften the loss of my first.

Although the pregnancy was considered high risk before, it was even more so with twins, so I was immediately put on bed rest until they were born. I didn't argue. I would do whatever I needed to do to give these babies every chance of being born healthy. At first, I was concerned about how I would continue to work and build RGII simultaneously. To my surprise, my employer was very understanding and accommodating.

Every possible provision was made for me to work from home. I would be free of the stress and pressure of the office and the commute across the Woodrow Wilson Bridge from Maryland into Virginia and would still be productive while performing my job remotely.

Bed rest turned out to be a blessing in disguise. I was able to work from my bed, fax machine on one side and phone on the other. Laptops weren't as available then as they are today, and my heavy Pentium 286 simply wouldn't fit on the bed, so I did work by hand. In between conference calls with my staff and daily fetal monitoring with the hospital team, I had dedicated time to finish up the business plan.

The time came to start sending the plan out in search of the financing we needed to grow RGII into a self-sustaining business. I didn't intend to continue working for the government contractor any longer than I had to. We blanketed banks in Maryland, Virginia, and Washington, D.C., with the business plan. I wasn't optimistic, given start-ups' low rate of securing funding, but I was determined to find a way to get the money we needed.

A PUSH OUT THE DOOR

For the next few months, I led my work team from home, handling situations that came up to my boss's satisfaction, while my belly grew bigger by the day. However, by the summer of 1993, he was eager for my return. In June 1993, he asked when I thought I would be coming back to work.

From my perspective, his inquiry was extremely insensitive and premature. My number-one priority at that time was protecting and nurturing my soon-to-be-born babies, who weren't due until August, and he knew that. The understanding and flexibility my employer had shown early on in my pregnancy began to dissipate. Additionally, given that I had two months before my due date and 12 weeks of leave (under the Family Medical Leave Act) following their birth, I wouldn't realistically return until December. Why was he pushing for a return date so soon? His questioning reinforced that I no longer belonged at the company.

Exactly four weeks later, on July 29, 1993, my two miracles, Brya Simone and Brynn Nicole, were born four weeks premature, 5 lb., 1 oz., and 3 lb., 9 oz., respectively. I call them my miracles because the same septate uterus that prevented Little Greg from growing made it possible for both girls to grow, independently, each on their own side of the wall. By the grace and mercy of God, both girls were born healthy—two beautiful girls who are now tenth-grade honor students.

But back in 1993, following an 11-day hospital stay, Greg and I weren't exactly sure how we were going to raise twins on a limited income while trying to start a business. The babies helped put things into perspective, however, and I decided not to return to my full-time job. I knew my future success lay with RGII, and that's where I needed to invest my time and energy—when I wasn't caring for twin babies, that is. I knew I needed to take a leap of faith in order for the company to be successful.

Bootstrapping

I calculated that the pay from my former job and our savings would last us at least through the end of the year. I was officially an entrepreneur. To me, that meant "risk": taking a chance on losing everything that we had worked so hard for with the hope that we could build a company that would be successful beyond our wildest dreams. My parents always told me, "Nothing beats a failure but a try." I was ready to try, with my fallback plan being that I would return to full-time employment if we failed—but I wasn't focusing on failure, only on succeeding.

At that point, we had started receiving rejection letters from banks regarding the loan applications we had submitted, frequently citing our lack of collateral or high debt ratio as the reason for being declined. This went on for months. In fact, we received one letter on our ninth wedding anniversary, June 1! While it did initially put a damper on the celebration, we would not be deterred. One thing rang clear: the rejection letters certainly bolstered our contention on our 8(a) application that we were economically disadvantaged. Without the loan, we would be unable to cover our expenses.

Although the SBA claimed to be able to "fast-track" the 8(a) application process, that is, providing notice of acceptance or rejection within
90 days or sooner, the fast track wasn't fast enough for an anxious
entrepreneur betting on acceptance to the program.

With bank rejection letters abound and our personal bank account
hovering around $3,000, all we had left were the credit cards, which
quickly became our funding source. The strategy was to draw cash
advances from the cards to pay our expenses, both personal and business. We may have had insufficient collateral and too much debt, but
we had plenty of credit available—$50,000 to be exact.

TAPPING INTO OUR AVAILABLE CREDIT/ACCESS TO CAPITAL

Using credit card debt to finance the business was the only source of
funding available at the time, though it was certainly not my first choice.
In fact, under normal circumstances, it would have been my next-to-last
resort. The last resort would certainly have been a move of desperation,
cashing in my 401(k) plan, valued at $20,000. At the time, I wasn't
ready or willing to do that yet; it was all we had left. Without credit
cards, the company simply could not have been launched because we
had no other funds.

The limits on the credit cards we had ranged from $5,000 to $10,000,
and we had multiple cards from which to choose. I devised a spending
plan to take advantage of the cash advance feature available on each
card. With the cash advances, I covered our personal expenses, such as
the mortgage, food, and child care for the twins, and I used the charge
feature to pay business expenses, such as travel, parking, brochures,
and business cards. In fact, I had to use the cash advances from one
card to pay the amount due on another, masterfully juggling our credit
with careful attention to every detail. One misstep could put us in a bad
credit position.

In order to qualify for a traditional small-business loan, we needed
tangible assets that could be used as collateral, such as contracts,
accounts receivable, equipment, or real estate. Although we owned a

home we had purchased in 1987 that could have been collateralized, the banks didn't think it was enough.

I submitted more than 100 business plans to 100 banks in the region and was turned down by every one of them for one or more of the following reasons: insufficient collateral, insufficient cash flow, debt too high, and/or the business was a risky investment. (Of course it was a risky investment; it was a start-up!) In fact, studies have shown that minority-owned small businesses do face restrictions in access to capital. Research reported in the Federal Reserve Board's 1998 National Survey on Small Business Finances showed that "African American and Hispanic-owned firms face significantly greater loan denial probability than white male firm owners." Of course, this did not take me by surprise. However, I was still faced with restricted access to working capital I so desperately needed. Access to capital is critical to the success of budding entrepreneurs, and going without severely cripples their growth.

What I quickly realized in dealing with the banks was that they had zero tolerance for risk. While they might have been great supporters of entrepreneurship in theory, in practice it was far too risky for them to underwrite—which is probably why 39.1% of small businesses surveyed in 1993 by the Federal Reserve Board as part of its National Survey of Small Business Finances reported using personal credit cards to finance new and expanding businesses. What else did they have? Few traditional banks were willing to lend to small businesses back then.

Interestingly, while banks have now realized the potential for growth that small businesses provide and the lucrative market segment that it is, few changes appear to have occurred on the lending front. Ten years later, the same survey revealed that in 2003, more than 77% of small businesses used either a business credit card or a personal credit card to pay for business expenses. Part of this change had to do with the advantages of using credit cards for necessary business purchases, but the other part of the story is that credit cards are still much easier to obtain than a traditional small-business loan. Access to capital remains a serious deterrent to small-business growth in the United States, and researching and considering creative alternatives have led entrepreneurs to look for unconventional sources.

ON THE PATH TO FINANCING

Looking back, there were a number of things we did right and others we could have done better, had we known what we know now. The path you take to determine the best funding source for your business is dictated by access to the sources of capital. Entrepreneurs can consider both traditional and nontraditional sources of funding, but first, I believe that what I term "housekeeping" should be tackled prior to throwing the nets out in the turbulent financing waters. Below is a discussion of what I see as the various elements of housekeeping.

Credit score. One advantage that we had from the onset of starting the company was excellent credit. Our A+ credit rating gave us access to varying interest rate credit cards that we effectively used to fund the company.

One caution: before applying for every credit card you can get your hands on, make sure that you know what's in your credit report. Everyone is entitled to a free copy of his or her credit report each year. You should request one at www.annualcreditreport.com and check it over thoroughly. Correct any errors and do what you can to improve your credit score immediately. Why is your credit score important? As an entrepreneur/business owner, your personal credit score is what is used by most banks, if not all, to determine your creditworthiness and their potential risk exposure. For banks with a small portfolio of small-business loans, this score becomes even more important when evaluating loan applications. Having a strong credit score will make credit cards and loans easier to obtain.

Tolerance for risk. Understanding how much risk you are willing to take with your business venture is a critical housekeeping item. Being an entrepreneur is all about risk: risk of going into uncharted waters, financial instability, family and personal relationship pressures, risk of failure, and even the risk of succeeding. Being risk averse, which I was initially, should in no way be the sole determining factor in your decision. However, the assessment of how much risk you are willing to take and how much skin you are willing to put in the game, while understanding not only the upside but also the potential downside, is not an easy one to make—but make it you must.

Banking relationship. One area where we were at a disadvantage was in not having a personal relationship with our banker/account manager when we first went to apply for a loan. This delayed funding and hurt us initially.

I came to learn that the whole process of landing a small-business loan would have been far easier if we had established a personal relationship with the manager of our local bank early on, which we didn't know to do. Although banks are still risk averse, especially when they don't understand your industry, having a close working relationship with your branch manager is a step in the right direction. Keep him or her up-to-date on what's going on with your business and share your finances along the way so that when the time comes for you to apply for an expansion loan, you have a relationship that will give you a much better chance of hearing a "yes." Because the bank manager now understands where you've been and how you've built the business, he or she will recognize the low level of risk where others perceive it to be greater. Educating the banker, an actual person of interest—not the institution—about your company and where it is headed can save you considerable time and energy down the road.

Keep in mind that some banks just won't get it. You need to be able to recognize this and work around it. One place we applied was the local branch of a major national bank that not only held our business account but also had advertised its support for small businesses. I won't mention the name here, but believe me, you know it. The bank representative who was assigned to work with us looked through our business plan and spotted the problem immediately. He stated, "The problem here is you are growing too quickly." How could that be, with three employees and no working capital? It was lunacy at best. His solution was to slow our business development (BD) efforts in order to improve our odds of having our loan application approved.

Not only was his solution absurd but also his advice confirmed that he didn't understand our business plan or where we were headed as a company. Who tells a growing company to halt BD and growth in order to have a loan approved? Needless to say, we ended that relationship and found a new one with a small local bank, Annapolis National Bank, now Bank Annapolis. Our new bank not only welcomed our account but also facilitated our application for an SBA-backed low-documentation (low-doc) loan, which the SBA would guarantee up to 80%. Today, it is possible to get a 90% guarantee on some small business loans and a 100% on micro loans. In our case, we were approved for a $50,000 loan with my personal guarantee and the SBA's backing—but not before being forced to make the desperate move of cashing in my 401(k) to make payroll for three new employees who were hired to support a new client at the Federal Aviation Administration (FAA), our first funded contract. That was the week that Greg and I had only $300 left in our bank account and bankruptcy was looking more and more appealing.

The loan process was tedious at best and drawn out at worst. However, the loan allowed us to eventually wean ourselves off credit cards as a means of financing the company, and it put us on a growth trajectory from that point forward.

Eventually, we would be in the fortunate position of having banks approach us with offers of lines of credit and other financing tools. But it took even longer—only after we had generated more than $10 million in revenue—before we would be exempt from personally guaranteeing such debt.

If we had introduced ourselves early on and had begun developing a working relationship with our account manager, informing him about our growth strategy and including him as a silent partner, the more likely we would have been to secure the small loan we needed more quickly. Maybe we wouldn't have experienced some of the challenges I described earlier in this chapter. I did, however, learn early on that the best time to develop a banking relationship is when you don't need it, so that when you do, getting what you need is easier. The right bank and the right account manager are integral components to obtaining financing when the company needs it most.

Willingness to give up ownership. One decision that seriously limited our options for financing was that I was unwilling to give up ownership in RGII. Having left an unsatisfactory employment situation and risked everything to run my own show, I certainly did not want to give anyone else the opportunity to take control of my future.

Although my unwillingness to give up an ownership stake in exchange for needed capital limited my options, I still believe that it was the right decision for me. Every entrepreneur has to make this decision at some point, and the basis for that decision is determined solely by the business owner. Take a hard look at your overall objectives and willingness to relinquish some portion of the company to others; it is a personal decision that you and your advisors together should make. If you ultimately decide that split ownership is right for you, make sure that you clearly understand what you are giving up in exchange for the investment, i.e., majority ownership or a smaller ownership position. Ownership position becomes key if your strategy involves government-related programs such as the 8(a) program. Under this program, the owner has to maintain 51% ownership in the company to qualify and be eligible for ongoing participation.

While our funding options were limited, I don't want you to get the idea that there are only two or three sources of funding. In fact, there are several. The following are the most common.

Friends and family. The biggest advantage of borrowing from friends and family is that they know you well—in some cases, maybe too well, and then this option could become a disadvantage. One of the upsides to friends and family is that you can better negotiate a flexible repayment schedule. That can be a pivotal milestone for many entrepreneurs, especially in the early cash-crunched days. The downside, however, is that your family and friends may be in a similar financial situation, with limited resources available to tap into. If their resources are limited, the flexible schedule may be very short-term, which may not be as long as you need it to be. On the other hand, if they have resources to invest, the flexible repayment schedule could work to your advantage.

Some friends and family may have the means but may not be willing to risk their savings, despite the fact that they have full confidence in your abilities to start a successful company. They could see the risk as being too great for them to handle. In some cases, family relationships have been strained following the failure of a business or the inability of the entrepreneur to repay the funds on the agreed-upon timetable. Therefore, when accepting help from this group, you must understand the familial risk that is present, and you need to decide whether you are willing to put those relationships on the line for the sake of achieving your dream. Therefore, unless your circle of friends or your network consists of people with the financial means to invest in a venture such as yours, this potential funding source relationship should not be entered into lightly—somewhat like marriage.

Traditional bank loans. Bank loans, also referred to as term loans and lines of credit, continue to be the most sought-after forms of financing for small businesses. In fact, with these types of credit instruments, you have access to the approved amount up front, to use as needed. Fully understanding your credit terms and repayment schedule and adhering to the terms and conditions put you in a position of leverage. Leverage the relationship with the bank and the account manager to get more when the need arises.

Keep in mind our earlier discussion on credit scores. Your personal scores will be a key determinant of credit terms. They won't be the only determining factor, but they do play a large role in securing not only the amount that you need but also the terms that you can live with. Let's not forget that most banks are highly risk averse and want to see collateral and a solid credit capacity; depending on your current financial position, this may indeed be a viable option. As with all financing options, having a champion on your side who is fighting for a favorable outcome for you puts you in a better position for potential success.

Credit cards. I touched on my credit card use to fund the company earlier in this chapter. I would simply add here that personal credit cards typically carry interest rates upward of 15%, while business credit card interest rates are slightly lower and more competitive. However, credit cards continue to be one of the most expensive financing options, and I was forced to use all of mine. They serve as a revolving line of credit, and if you can manage the payments, credit cards are an increasingly popular tool, especially for entrepreneurs who can't access traditional funding sources right away. I caution those considering using credit cards to be careful, however; they are easy to get and use but can also quickly lead to more financial difficulties.

Second mortgage/home equity line of credit (HELOC). Although Greg and I didn't want to tap into the small amount of equity in our home or put ourselves at risk of losing it when we started RGII, using available home equity is one way to extract cash from an existing personal asset. A home equity loan or line of credit, also referred to as a second mortgage, allows you to borrow money by using your home's equity as collateral. The amount of equity available in your home is the difference between what your home is worth and what you owe, or the remaining balance on the mortgage. Let's look at an example.

———————————————— EXAMPLE ————————————————

At the time that I needed capital to finance the company, we lived in our home for six years and made all scheduled payments consistently on time, which meant that we had six years of equity available. To illustrate how to calculate how much equity you may have in your home, let's take a home purchased six years ago for $200,000. After making timely monthly payments, six years later the balance remaining on the mortgage is $185,000. You have successfully paid down your mortgage by $15,000.

In order to apply for a home equity loan/line of credit, your home must be appraised to determine its current value. For this example, say the home was appraised for $350,000 during an up market, signaling a significant increase in the value of the home. This homeowner now has $165,000 of home equity available to borrow against to help fund the company.

Home Loan Amount/Purchase Price	$200,000
Six years later:	
Purchase Price	$200,000
Less Principal Payments	- 15,000
Remaining Balance	$185,000
Current Appraised Value	$350,000
Less Remaining Balance	- 185,000
Home Equity Available	$165,000

Banks prefer home equity lines to small-business loans because of the available collateral that more than covers the value of the debt you are pursuing. Once again, as in other financing options, approach such debt cautiously and with full knowledge of the terms and conditions. In the best-case scenario, the equity will provide the cash boost the company needs, but in the worst case, you could lose your home during a business cash crunch. The best advice I have for you is to know what you're getting into and seek professional advice.

Angel investors. Some entrepreneurs, especially those with a need for large amounts of cash, will turn to outside investors for potential cash infusions. Pursuing angel investors takes knowledge and business savvy. Most investors at this level have money to invest and the business and management know-how to spot a good investment. Although angel investors assume great risk when investing, they typically invest in start-ups and other small businesses with new leading-edge technologies, and they seek high returns, upward of 10 times their investment, usually in short order (generally fewer than five years).

The benefit of taking on investors is that they have available cash to invest and valuable experience and contacts that can benefit your business. However, in exchange for their cash infusion, you may have to relinquish some percentage of ownership in your company. That is more common with equity and venture capital financing, which will be discussed later.

Most angel investors are not interested in taking over your company or playing a management role. Many seek to mentor up-and-coming small businesses that have high growth potential and then exit at an agreed-upon time as their returns are achieved. Angel investors have become so widespread that they are organizing themselves into groups. One such group is Active Capital, formerly ACE-NET. Active Capital is a listing service that provides information to private investors on promising small businesses seeking to raise $250,000 to $5 million in equity financing. It is sponsored by the SBA's Office of Advocacy. Learn more about the members of the Active Capital network by visiting www.activecapital.org. As with all financing options, do your research, gain knowledge, and seek professional advice from an attorney or accountant before signing on the dotted line.

Private equity/venture capital. Most private equity and venture capitalists are interested in companies that are technology based, with some innovative product or service that has the potential for rapid growth and profitability with expected return within five to seven years. Both private equity and venture capital are available from firms that specialize in financing start-up, early development, and expansion of growth companies in return for equity, or ownership.

This form of financing is costly. In fact, with this option, you are guaranteed to give up an ownership position to the investor, and you may also have outside management involvement, depending on the amount of the investment. Deciding how much ownership you are willing to divest yourself of is a decision not to be taken lightly. I stated earlier that I was not willing to give up ownership, which caused me much angst by bootstrapping and taking out small-business loans, but that was my strategy. In other circumstances, it can work out just fine.

One thing to keep in mind is that if your strategy entails government programs, as in my case, you must maintain majority ownership, that is, 51%, to qualify for these programs. Be certain that you do your homework before selling a majority stake in your company in exchange for the coveted capital investment. Additional information on private equity/venture capital sources can be found at www.nvca.org.

GOVERNMENT-SPONSORED/BACKED PROGRAMS

Small Business Investment Companies (SBICs). The SBIC program was created by Congress in 1958 and is licensed by the Small Business Administration. All SBICs are privately owned and managed investment firms that possess their own funds and provide venture capital to start-ups and small established businesses. These investment companies are for-profit entities that invest in companies that have the opportunity for growth and success. In addition to receiving equity and loans, companies also have access to expert management advice from the SBIC member. Although SBICs are permitted to provide financing, they are restricted from permanently controlling an invested business. SBA holds approved SBICs to strict guidelines in order to eliminate conflicts of interest. A complete listing of SBA-approved SBICs can be found at www.sba.gov.

Small Business Innovation Research (SBIR) Grants. SBIR grants are another source of funding if your small business is developing some form of product. The SBIR program was created by the Small Business Administration during the early 1980s to stimulate innovation, primarily technological in nature, by funding research and development (R&D) projects using small businesses. Grants of this nature can cover the cost of R&D, which is not normally an affordable expense for most companies and has the potential to eat away at company profits. Although SBIR grants do not have to be repaid, payments are issued over three phases of the project. If you are successful and are awarded a grant of this nature, know that the process is slow and it could take months for you to receive the funding. Therefore, alternative funding is necessary.

The good thing about SBIR grants is that you don't have to repay them, even if your project flops. However, if your project succeeds, you have gained instant credibility, which puts you in a position to receive future grants or other types of financing from possible investors. More information on SBIR grants can be found at http://www.sba.gov/SBIR.

Other ways to reduce your cash outlay—perhaps while you continue to explore additional resources for needed cash infusion—include the following.

Leases. An oftentimes overlooked form of financing is leasing. Leasing refers to asset-based financing and is the most popular way to finance all types of business assets, including equipment, computers, printers, business machinery, vehicles, and even office furniture. All of these items depreciate in value and can be returned when the lease terms expire. However, most leasing agreements will have a provision that allows for purchase of the leased item at the end of the term. I caution you to weigh this option carefully because equipment has a way of becoming obsolete and purchasing the now-used equipment may not offer you long-term strategic value.

What leasing does is free up working capital to be used for other pressing matters of business. In the beginning, we leased everything because the company was short on working capital and an outright investment in equipment was not possible. Under the leasing option, you or your attorney negotiates a lease term with a reputable leasing company, found through the Internet or Yellow Pages, and pays a monthly fee in exchange for the use of the equipment. The equipment itself serves as collateral, therefore requiring little or no money up front. Keep in mind that the leasing terms you are able to secure are also driven by the company's or individual owner's credit standing. That sends us back to the importance of maintaining a good credit history and the importance of adhering to the credit terms without imposing undue financial burden on the company. Note that leased equipment, although depreciable, can't be classified as a depreciable asset on your books. You may, however, deduct the lease payments and receive a tax benefit. Be sure to consult your accountant on the proper way to record the payments.

Factoring. Once we had receivables due us from our contracts, we used a financing method called factoring. Factoring is a financing source whereby the company's accounts receivable (monies owed the company by customers) become the asset being leveraged. In this case, the lender, say, a bank or other factoring company, purchases your receivable (invoice or invoices) in exchange for an advanced payment of a percentage of the invoice. For example, receivables due from customers X and Y amount to $50,000 and are due to be paid in 30 days, per the agreed-upon payment terms. However, in order to have working capital available for operating expenses, you need cash within the next 10 days. With factoring, the lender advances 75%–90% of the total value of your receivables and charges a fee of 2% or more for that advance. The remaining balance of the receivables will be released upon receipt by the lender of full payment of the outstanding receivables/invoices.

Yes, factoring can be expensive, but if you need working capital to make payroll, buy needed equipment, or pay other expenses, it is worth the extra cost if traditional funding sources are not readily available. While factoring won't work to generate start-up funds, it can be a useful short-term financing instrument, especially during a period of growth.

Incubator space/access. Small-business incubators are buildings or facilities that are made available for the developing entrepreneur and start-up companies. Incubators provide a nurturing environment and invaluable assistance and resources during a time when start-up companies are most vulnerable. The level of assistance and available resources is dependent on the size of the incubator. However, most incubators provide the same type of services to their residents: services such as access to affordable shared office space, inexpensive leases, equipment, conference facilities, and administrative support staff may be part of the package.

In addition, incubators provide valuable business resources such as consultants with expertise in business planning, marketing and sales, and access to financing via financial partners. Incubators should not be considered for the long term. In fact, you should have a definite exit strategy, whereby you are preparing for one day being able to leave the security of the incubator and obtain your own lease for commercial space. To find an incubator in your state, visit the National Business Incubator Association (NBIA) Web site at http://www.nbia.org/resource_center/links_to_member_incubators/index.php. NBIA is considered to be the world's leading organization for advancing business incubators and entrepreneurship.

The good news is that today capital *is* available—you just have to know where to look. Once you have done your research and located the source, be ready to tell your business story effectively. Be able to clearly articulate the business and why it is a promising investment for the would-be investor. What will the return on investment be, and when will it be available? This plays into your vision for the company and your ability to lead the company in achieving the goals and objectives you have set. If you're just starting out, you may not have the long track record that other companies may have, but leverage what you do have to obtain the financing you need. As your company grows and becomes profitable, believe me, funding sources will come looking for you. Then you get to be in the driver's seat, accepting or rejecting the myriad offers put in front of you.

Lessons Learned

The ability to obtain financing validates the entrepreneur and the business venture. Without it, the dream won't become a reality.

☑ Start talking now to your local bank manager about your plans, even before you've officially started your business. Share your business plan, your market research, your long-term intentions. Then, drop in every once in a while to keep him or her informed of your progress. You'll significantly improve your odds of being approved for a loan if the manager has witnessed all you've accomplished to that point.

(continued on page 57)

LESSONS LEARNED
(continued from page 56)

☑ Although credit card debt should not be your preferred means of financing your start-up, because of the high interest rates associated with such borrowing, you will certainly be in the majority if you find you have to go that route. Business use of credit cards to fund operations is now quite commonplace. Just be careful not to borrow too heavily or even that tool will be unavailable to you.

☑ Taking on an equity partner, meaning an angel investor or private equity firm, will yield money you won't have to pay back, but you will have to give up an ownership stake in exchange for the investment. Think long and hard about whether you're willing to relinquish control in order to achieve faster growth.

☑ Some financing sources are more risky than others but probably not for the reasons you think. Turning to family and friends, although considered the easiest avenue, can lead to misunderstanding, friction, and turmoil down the road. Likewise, a second mortgage or home equity loan will get you money fast, but you're putting yourself at risk of losing your home should you get behind in your loan repayment.

☑ If you have an income stream, bootstrapping your company's growth is commonplace. However, with this method, keeping costs low and reducing expenses will be critical so you are not overextending your personal finances to cover business-related expenses.

☑ Leases are one way to get the equipment you need without an upfront outlay of cash. Factoring can turn accounts receivable into instant cash very quickly.

☑ The best time to seek financing is when you don't need it.

CHAPTER 4

TAPPING INTO GOVERNMENT PROGRAMS

*"So I say to you: Ask and it will be given to you; seek and you
will find; knock and the door will be opened to you."*
— *Luke 11:9*

With our 8(a) participation confirmed and our loan in place, we began to start marketing in earnest. Back then, our marketing campaign consisted of passing out brochures in as many small-business offices within Washington, D.C., federal agencies as we could identify. By "small-business offices" I mean the Office of Small Disadvantaged Business Utilization (OSDBU), which each and every federal agency has. The role of the OSDBU is to serve as an advocate for small businesses within the respective agency, assisting and supporting them as much as possible in learning how to pursue agency contracts. The OSDBU was our foot in the door.

The purchasing, or procurement, process at most agencies is not the same. However, despite the different processes, what was available then—and still is today—was a vast amount of contracting opportunities, both small and large, and a wealth of information to help us plot our path.

Each federal agency's OSDBU offers a free information packet titled "Doing Business with ..." that includes step-by-step instructions on identifying the proper point of contact within the organization for the type of products and services you sell. It also includes information about the agency's mission and budget for the fiscal year, which runs October 1 to September 30. The budget information can be particularly helpful because it indicates exactly what the agency anticipates purchasing within that fiscal year. Depending on the amount budgeted, the business can then determine whether that agency is a good fit for its marketing efforts.

The U.S. government buys just about everything: office supplies and cleaning supplies, food and clothing, aircraft carriers, consulting services, computers, furniture, publications—you name it. It is worth it to your business to assess and discover which agency holds the greatest opportunity for you because not all agencies have the same purchasing needs.

Our company's initial offerings were program management and computer services, and our initial target government customers were the Department of Transportation, specifically, the Federal Aviation Administration (FAA); the Department of Commerce, specifically, the

National Oceanic and Atmospheric Administration (NOAA); and the Department of Navy's Naval Sea Systems Command and Naval Supply Systems Command.

Given that the federal government has easily more than 100 agencies, we knew that there was no way we could target all of them and be successful. The company was too new and too small to spread our marketing resources—meaning Greg's and my time—across so many potential customers. We decided to zero in on the agencies most likely to have requirements for IT-related services rather than attempting to market to all of them. By focusing our efforts and developing detailed marketing plans for each of the five agencies we intended to pursue, we increased our probability of winning business from them.

HELP FROM THE SBA

Fortunately, by virtue of our participation in the 8(a) program, we also had help from a Business Opportunity Specialist (BOS) assigned by the SBA's Baltimore, Maryland, office, where our case file resided. The role of the BOS was to serve as the primary point of contact with the SBA should we have questions or need guidance regarding 8(a) opportunities. Our BOS, Mrs. Sandra Crawford, was extremely helpful in outlining how the 8(a) program actually worked and how we could get a leg up on available contracts within the agencies we had targeted.

We first met Mrs. Crawford in our new shared office in Annapolis, Maryland's state capital, which is located about 30 minutes in either direction between Washington, D.C., and Baltimore. The office wasn't ideal—we shared it with an architect whose workspace was above a beauty salon—but it was all we could afford at the time. We had decided it was time to move up and out of the basement and into commercial space.

That first meeting was a bit nerve-wracking for me because I didn't know how she would react to the very meager surroundings we were working in; we had a desk, a phone, a file box, and not much else. This was all we had, so there was nothing I could do about it, but I was still nervous about the first impression RGII Technologies was making on her.

To our surprise, she wasn't at all shocked or disappointed by our surroundings, quickly telling us that she had seen worse. Relieved, we sat down to discuss how we could best use the 8(a) program to secure contracts with the federal government.

Mrs. Crawford explained how the 8(a) program worked, how it could benefit RGII if approached properly, and what our respective responsibilities were. She made it very clear that we would not be receiving phone calls from the SBA telling us that it had found a contract for us and to come down and sign it. That's not how it worked, she explained. However, if we used the program the way it was designed, as a self-marketing business development tool that would give us access to federal contracts set aside for 8(a) participants, and if we performed well on the contracts we won, we would do well in the program and be prepared to graduate in nine years. What she meant was that every company graduates in nine years, but some are better prepared than others to pursue government contracts on the open market, without the 8(a) benefits.

Our responsibility was to market RGII Technologies to the federal government the same way we marketed to corporate customers: by making phone calls, setting up meetings, knocking on doors, and pounding the pavement. We had to sell our potential clients on why RGII was the best company for the job, what our value proposition was, and how the client would benefit by awarding the contract to us versus our competitor—not just because we were an 8(a) company but because of the superior products and services we could provide.

Before she left, Mrs. Crawford handed me an 8(a) program handbook and a guide to selling to the federal government, which she encouraged me to read thoroughly. She also recommended that we get a copy of the Code of Federal Regulation (CFR) (www.gpoaccess.gov/cfr/index.html) and the Federal Acquisition Regulation (FAR) (www.arnet.gov/far), the bibles on doing business with the government.

At the time, back in the early 1990s, doing business with an 8(a) company was very attractive to government agencies. Finding a suitable business from which to purchase products and services through the 8(a) program was one of the fastest ways to issue a contract without having to go through an extensive competitive bidding process. In fact, a contract could be awarded to an 8(a) company without competition, which is referred to as a sole-source award. A sole-source award is the Holy Grail in many ways: being awarded a contract without any kind of competition at all. Unfortunately, several strong 8(a) companies operated in our midst, and we would come up against them regularly in the bidding process during the next nine years. Sole-source awards were few and far between as a result.

After our discussion with Mrs. Crawford, Greg and I pushed ahead with an aggressive marketing plan while we worked hard to secure our first contract. To enhance our odds, we invested in a new, slicker capabilities brochure. It was still sparse, but it told our story in a professional manner. Greg also began reaching into his Rolodex, making contact with past acquaintances who might be able to support our contracting goals.

One of those acquaintances was Dr. Herman Rhett, a consultant who had previously supported Department of Transportation programs and who was excited to hear about what our new company was doing. Knowing that we needed someone with his expertise to be able to pursue and successfully complete contracts, we offered him a position with RGII. We couldn't offer him a huge salary at the time, but we did promise challenges and future rewards in which we would all share. He accepted and committed to winning a contract for the company within 90 days.

By that time, we were making enough money to afford an office of our own, which we found a mile away. It was a total of 710 square feet, just enough space for Greg, Dr. Rhett, and me. Because we couldn't yet afford a receptionist, I multitasked and handled those duties in addition to my others.

OUR BIG BREAK

For months, Greg had been talking with a talented engineer named Patrick Sweeney about pursuing a potential opportunity at the FAA's technical center in New Jersey. We needed Pat, who had worked with this particular agency and client before, in order to be seriously considered. We had tried marketing our services to the FAA ourselves with no luck but knew of the opportunities there based on the agency's forecasted contract report.

Although the client was not familiar with RGII, it had worked with Pat extensively and was confident in his technical and engineering background and his familiarity with the FAA systems. As a result, we hired him and were awarded the contract for engineering services. This was a huge break for us, and we wanted to make the most of it by doing everything right.

We started by assessing the contract requirements. Our first task was to perform what is referred to as "shakedown testing" on aviation systems. In layman's terms, that meant we had to simulate in a closed environment the landing and takeoff of aircraft and the impact on landing and takeoff when certain unexpected factors were introduced, such as wind, rain, or turbulence, for example.

Personally, I had never heard of shakedown testing and hadn't the slightest idea of how to do it, but Pat did, and that was why we had hired him. With his understanding of the task and the client's needs, we quickly determined how to approach the work. First, we needed to locate engineers with the required expertise and hire them to help with this contract. Fortunately, that didn't take long because a whole team was performing the same task for another company right down the hall. Convincing them to join our start-up did take a bit longer. We didn't have a lot of the benefits that other companies had to offer, so we emphasized the momentum, growth opportunities, and excitement of working in a new venture. It worked. We had a team of engineers now at work on our FAA contract.

Another key member of the team was the contracting officer (CO) for the FAA. Both tough and fair, she taught me everything I needed to know about the dos and don'ts of government contracting. As the agency official authorized to develop, enter into, and administer contracts on behalf of the FAA, she was watching out for her agency's best interests—and mine—as she drove home a few points about how I needed to work.

First, the CO insisted that I understand the requirements of the contract itself, discerning what accurate and timely deliverables meant, and she emphasized the importance of accurate invoices that reflected the actual hours worked by each employee. She pointed out that a mistake on any of those items could delay our payments, and recognizing the importance of cash flow to a small business, she wanted to ensure that we were paid as promptly as possible. These were all useful pieces of information, but the most important lesson she taught me was to listen closely and work to understand the individual needs of each client. By partnering with each client to create solutions that yielded measurable, beneficial results for the federal government, we would solidify a positive performance history.

Notice that I draw a distinction between a customer and a client. I contend that customers are those who buy something from you once, or perhaps a few times, because you had it available for them. Yours is a transactional relationship, not ongoing. Clients, on the other hand, seek your business out because of the professional advice and expertise you can provide, because of how you help them find solutions. With clients, you build and cultivate long-standing relationships that benefit you both by your mutual enhanced experiences and results. By making your company the go-to firm for your clients, you become a value-added partner, and both your reputation and your client base will grow exponentially.

LEVERAGING ONE CONTRACT TO GET OTHERS

The business plan I had written for RGII called for the company to generate $1.0 million in revenue by year-end 1995—a stretch goal but one we were committed to achieving. On December 31, we closed the books with revenue of $1,005,000, a figure slightly above our goal. That $1-million milestone was important for the company and became the springboard for greater growth to come.

Within months of winning the FAA contract, we won another contract, this time with the National Oceanic and Atmospheric Administration (NOAA), the largest agency under the auspices of the Department of Commerce. On the basis of our performance history and contacts made within the agency, we won this help desk contract on a limited competition basis.

The contract was to provide tier 1 help desk support to users working within the Systems Acquisition Office. To meet the terms of the contract, we needed to significantly increase our computer and IT services capability, a stepping-stone that was good for our company in many ways. We hired two people who were instrumental in getting the contract awarded to RGII and, in turn, recommended others who would round out the remaining members of the help desk team.

The CO on this contract was the late Jay Moore. Like our CO on the FAA contract, he was tough. Unfortunately, he was even tougher and more demanding. There was no gray area with Jay. However, knowing this proved beneficial. It helped in determining how best to serve him as a client, but it also made for stressful work days.

Fortunately, with the two key hires we made, one as vice president responsible for the Networks and Information Technology Solutions business unit and the other as program manager, I assured him that he had nothing to worry about—and he didn't. During the next nine years, Jay became a strong supporter of RGII and was instrumental in the growth of our business within NOAA.

That growth also created some challenges. We quickly outgrew our 716-square-foot office space, so we expanded by 100% into space within the same building. In fact, we would expand three times on the same floor over the next five years, from 716 to 7,000 square feet. I had decided early on that we would never be in the real estate business, so we moved into larger office space as growth dictated but never with the goal of owning our own building.

UNDERSTANDING SET-ASIDES

The growth of our company was due primarily to the quality of our workers and our commitment to learning about and meeting our clients' needs, but our access to set-asides was no small advantage at the outset. Set-asides are government contracts that can be bid on by a designated group of companies, i.e., small businesses, 8(a) participants, minority/

women/veteran owned, etc. Such contracts are made possible by the Small Business Set-Aside Program and administered by the CO for each agency; each CO determines which contracts meet the requirements necessary to be set aside.

Namely, if a contract is valued between $2,500 and $100,000, it is routinely set aside for competition between small businesses and 8(a) companies. Contracts over $100,000 may also be set aside if the CO is confident that at least two small businesses/8(a) companies are qualified and willing to bid. Contracts under $2,500 may not be set aside. Another option that COs have available is the partial set-aside, where portions of larger contracts may be separated, making it more manageable and likely that a small business could successfully tackle a piece of the larger pie.

The first step in exploring set-asides is becoming certified as a small, minority-owned, woman-owned, socially and economically disadvantaged, or veteran-owned business. Certification is a paperwork-filled process designed to confirm or refute your contention that your company is small and owned by someone who is economically or socially disadvantaged. If you can document such facts, you should have no trouble earning certification; you need only suffer through the reams of documents required.

While some corporations allow small businesses to self-certify, meaning that they sign on a dotted line and promise that they meet the definition of minority owned, woman owned, small, etc., government agencies require more proof. They want a third party to check you out, which means that you'll need to work with either a state agency or a national organization that provides such certification.

To learn more about becoming certified, start with your state's Department of Business and Economic Development, one of the many government resources about which you'll want to know more.

In addition, many organizations and agencies are available to serve small businesses on local, state, and national levels. Depending on your location, industry, and business goals, you will find most if not all of these resources to be valuable.

Small-Business Resources

Whether your goal is to serve a government, nonprofit, industrial, commercial, or consumer customer base, many government-sponsored or government-funded organizations and agencies exist to help small businesses get started and succeed. Most offer consulting services at no charge, though some do charge a nominal fee. Some also provide reference materials, such as directories, workbooks, pamphlets, spreadsheets, or booklets.

Some are operated on a national level, while others are overseen at the state or local level. Depending on your business goals and geographic focus, you may find one type of organization more useful to you than another.

Nationally

U.S. Small Business Administration. In my efforts to finish my business plan, I turned first to the Small Business Administration (SBA) (www.sba.gov), and I would suggest that you do the same if you haven't already. The SBA is a federal agency established specifically to assist small-business formation and growth. At the organization's Web site, you can read about the process of starting and growing a business and can take online courses in subjects ranging from starting a business, finance and accounting, and e-commerce to federal tax training and government contracting. Here you can also listen to small-business-related podcasts, subscribe to monthly Web chats, and download useful resource guides—all at no cost.

The SBA is the most comprehensive small-business agency, serving a broad cross section of small businesses, from established mom-and-pops to new technology start-ups and everything in between, including companies in crisis. It focuses slightly more on encouraging the creation of new businesses, however, and its available resources reflect that. You *will* find information appropriate for the established, growing venture, too, but it will likely be more general in nature. For specific guidance, you may be referred elsewhere, as we were.

Service Corps of Retired Executives (SCORE). What we needed initially was help in identifying the many opportunities available to small businesses such as ours, meaning programs for minority-owned businesses pursuing the federal government as their clients. Knowing that the U.S. government is the single largest purchaser of goods and services in the world, we thought it made perfect sense to go after such a large buyer; theoretically, our odds of earning some of the $300 billion (see http://www.sbtdc.org/SERVICES/sell_fedgov.asp) the government spends each year were fairly good.

The SBA referred us to the Service Corps of Retired Executives (SCORE) (www.score.org), an SBA-sponsored organization of more than 10,000 experienced business owners. These veteran entrepreneurs volunteer their time to help new companies get started and also assist business owners in overcoming obstacles they encounter along the way. More than eight million companies have benefited from their help, including RGII Technologies.

We requested and received one-on-one mentoring from an invaluable SCORE counselor who pointed us in the direction of the 8(a) program early on. To find an office that provides one-on-one mentoring or offers on-site seminars and workshops, search the organization's Web site using your zip code: http://www.score.org/findscore/index.html. At SCORE's Web site, you can also download articles, tips, and advice to help you better run your small business.

Small Business Development Center (SBDC). Sponsored by the SBA but frequently located on the campuses of U.S. colleges and universities, the 1,000 or so SBDC offices provide free consulting and low-cost training to entrepreneurs. To find one in your area, search the SBDC Web site, http://www.asbdc-us.org.

The SBDC's mission is to support the creation and retention of small businesses, which total more than 22 million, including more than 800,000 established in the past year alone. Anyone in the process of evaluating or considering a potential new business, rather than already engaged in the start-up process, should definitely start here to receive free help in assessing the business concept.

Minority Business Enterprise Centers (MBECs). Although we did not tap into the services available at our local MBEC office (www. mbda.gov), this is one place to start if you are a minority entrepreneur. Part of the U.S. Department of Commerce, the Minority Business Development Agency has as its mission the goal to support the growth of minority-owned businesses. That includes providing consulting, training, and downloadable materials, as well as assistance in pursuing government contracting opportunities. The government defines minorities as people of African American, Asian, Hispanic, Native American, or Pacific Island descent.

One area of the MBDA Web site provides a thorough overview of the many types of loans that small businesses can pursue, including microloans, term loans, asset-based financing, SBA and state loan programs, and more.

Minority Business Opportunity Centers (MBOCs). Not to confuse you, but there are also MBOCs, which provide a slightly different service from MBECs. MBOC offices were established to help minority-owned firms identify new business opportunities and then leverage available local, state, and national resources to obtain them. These agencies are all about growth and new businesses, and they limit their guidance on start-up issues such as financing and human resources. However, both are run by the MBDA.

Native American Business Enterprise Centers (NABECs). Under the umbrella of the Minority Business Development Agency, NABECs provide the same services as the MBDCs but work exclusively with Native American–owned businesses.

Women Business Centers (WBCs). Established to help women-owned businesses start up and thrive, the 115 WBCs nationwide provide counseling, advocacy, and training to women entrepreneurs. In addition, the Association of Women Business Centers also conducts research about women-owned businesses in support of the centers' work. To find your nearest WBC office, check http://www.sba.gov/idc/groups/public/documents/sba_program_office/sba_pr_wbc_ed.pdf.

Procurement Technical Assistance Center (PTAC). The Procurement Technical Assistance Program established 91 local PTACs to assist small businesses in learning more about the process of doing business with federal, state, and local governments. Counseling and training are provided at little or no cost to area business owners. From learning how to identify contracting opportunities to effectively completing bid documents and understanding the requirements of each job, procurement professionals at the PTAC offices can guide you through the process.

Each office holds training sessions and matchmaking events to connect you with government agencies in need of the products or services you sell. To find the one closest to you, check http://www.dla.mil/db/procurem.htm.

Export-Import Bank of the U.S. (Ex-Im Bank). The primary mission of Ex-Im Bank is to facilitate the export of U.S. goods internationally, which it does by assisting with the financing of such trades. While the agency does not serve small businesses specifically, any entrepreneur contemplating exporting overseas will want to contact Ex-Im Bank (www.exim.gov/smallbiz/index.html) to learn more about cross-border payments and practices.

Within Ex-Im Bank's small-business portal at the site, you can discover how far the U.S. government is willing to go to help you export goods and services internationally. Working with an Ex-Im Bank trade advisor, you can extend credit without worrying about issues of nonpayment, and you can obtain working capital loans to enable your business to successfully fulfill any export contracts you win.

HUB zones. In 1997, the HUB Zone Empowerment Contracting Program was created by the SBA to provide incentives for companies that operate within historically underutilized business (HUB) zones. These areas of economic distress aren't always where you think they would be; some are pockets of a few square blocks surrounded by areas of activity.

The goal of the program is to rejuvenate neighborhoods by bringing economic activity back, often by encouraging businesses to relocate there through preference for government contracts, reduced taxes and rents, and assistance in hiring workers.

To qualify for HUB zone incentives, a company must be located within a HUB zone, be owned and operated by a U.S. citizen, and employ workers who live in the HUB zone (a minimum of 35% must live there).

HUB zone contracts can be one of three types: (1) sole source, if the contracting officer believes that only one responsive firm within the HUB zone can complete the work as specified; (2) competitive, if the contracting officer believes that at least two HUB zone companies are capable of meeting the terms of the contract; or (3) full and open competition with a price preference, meaning that anyone can bid but a HUB zone company's bid will be deemed lower than any others as long as its bid is no more than 10% higher than the rest.

To identify the HUB zones in your area, check the HUB zone map at http://map.sba.gov/hubzone/init.asp. Some local governments also provide incentives for businesses to set up shop within a HUB zone.

Economic development corporations. With a mission of attracting and creating new businesses, each state-level economic development corporation (EDC) offers information and incentives for existing companies to relocate and for new companies to develop within its borders. Those incentives may include tax abatements, training grants, funding assistance, support in identifying and hiring qualified workers, or other types of assistance. Each state's resources determine what it can offer small-business owners. In fact, in some states, the EDC is the certifying agency. To find your local economic development department, an internet search by county or state is the most efficient tool.

Chambers of commerce. Your area's chamber of commerce can be a critical point of contact for your business if you serve a local customer base. From market research to demographic information, traffic data, supplier names, and resource lists, the chamber of commerce can be a wealth of information. It can also provide networking opportunities that put you in touch with other area business owners.

Don't limit yourself solely to your zip code, however. Branch out and make contact with other chambers in your area. In addition to providing you with helpful business information, they can also be a potential referral source.

On a national level, the U.S. Chamber of Commerce (www.uschamber.com/sb/default.htm) offers a small-business library with downloadable workbooks and articles on topics such as hiring, sales and marketing, security, and shipping and delivery.

Although we started RGII with a stated goal of targeting and acquiring federal government agencies as our primary client base, you may have no interest in doing business with the federal government or, for that matter, the state or local government. That's fine. The resources I've just listed will be invaluable no matter what your target client base is.

LESSONS LEARNED

Government programs are funded with our tax dollars. These programs provide a hand up, not a hand out, so take full advantage of them whenever possible.

☑ The Small Business Administration (SBA) is a smart place to start in identifying organizations able to assist you in the start-up process. From there, you may be referred to other local, regional, or national agencies, such as SCORE, Small Business Development Centers, Minority Business Development Centers, Women Business Centers, Procurement Technical Assistance Centers, incubators, the Chamber of Commerce, the Economic Development Corporation, or other small-business-focused groups.

(continued on page 75)

LESSONS LEARNED
(continued from page 74)

☑ If you hope to pursue contracts with local, state, or federal government agencies, you'll want to consider applying for certification if you qualify. Becoming certified as a minority-owned, woman-owned, veteran-owned, or small and disadvantaged business will open doors to contracts you would not normally be qualified to bid on, which are termed set-asides.

☑ Should you decide to pursue government contracts, you'll want to review contracting guidelines for the agency you are approaching, as well as any information about "Doing Business with ..." Researching the agency's budget and percentage spent on your particular type of product or service should also be among your first steps to identify your best prospects.

☑ Every federal agency has a small-business advocate within its Office of Small Disadvantaged Business Utilization (OSDBU), which is where you should start your information gathering. Such officers can be extremely valuable in pointing you in the right direction and getting you the information you need.

☑ Even if you have no interest in pursuing government work, you should still take advantage of the free and low-cost help the government makes available to all of its citizens. Many organizations have been established specifically to aid in the creation and growth of small businesses.

CHAPTER 5

FINDING
AND RECRUITING
EMPLOYEES

"I waited patiently for the Lord: and he inclined unto me,
and heard my cry." — Psalms 40:1

I n the beginning, during the early years of RGII Technologies, I did everything myself. Most small-business owners do. I was the accounts payable and receivable departments, as well as the receptionist, sales division, and technical staff. But because my plan was to build a sizeable company in the federal government contractor marketplace, I knew that I couldn't do everything myself forever. Eventually, which was sooner than I expected, I would need to bring on help. The challenge for me, and for all business owners, really, was determining the right time.

It's a catch-22 situation. In order to grow, I, and many other small-business owners, needed more help. Yet until we grew, affording to pay for that help we needed would be nearly impossible.

Fortunately, in our case, we found someone who was willing to pitch in and help us on a volunteer basis. Octavia Petty came recommended by my brother-in-law, Charles Worthy, who recognized that I had maxed out what I could effectively accomplish in a given 24-hour period; he saw I was multitasking impressively but had hit a wall. I needed help, I told him, and he agreed. Unfortunately, I couldn't really afford to pay anyone, but I knew that I desperately needed a receptionist—cheap, I emphasized to Charles—and he suggested a friend who had recently retired after 31 years at the U.S. Department of Health and Human Services (HHS). She sounded marvelous. She turned out to be even better.

In addition to offering to volunteer her time until we were able to hire someone on a permanent basis, Octavia took charge of our administrative operations. Having worked as an executive secretary to the Deputy Assistant Secretary, Finance, at HHS for several decades, she taught me so much more than I taught her. Her first task was rearranging and reorganizing our tiny office.

Once she finished that, she took over rearranging how I worked.

"From this point forward, I will answer the phone, screen your calls, open the mail, keep your calendar, schedule your appointments, make any travel arrangements, maintain your Rolodex, make sure you take time to eat, help with your kids if needed, and do whatever necessary to remove unnecessary interruptions and stress," she informed me.

She wasn't kidding. Everyone quickly learned that Octavia was the gatekeeper; she determined whether I took a phone call or scheduled a meeting. Everyone who wanted to get to me had to get past her first. The smart ones quickly learned the importance of developing a relationship with her.

For the next 11 years, Octavia was my executive assistant, my right arm, my confidante, and my friend. She was my eyes and ears when I wasn't at the office, and she knew everything that went on, warning me of situations that might require my immediate attention. On occasion, she would notice when I wasn't in a good mood. She would say, "Are we having a bad day, Missy?" That statement would be followed by "You just need a neck rub," which she offered frequently.

She was the best first employee I could have hired. I only hope that every CEO can find someone who is as talented and professional and dedicated to your success as Octavia was to ours. Because of the bond we formed, she remains a very special and important person in my life.

WHAT IS YOUR PLAN?

Before you decide to take the giant leap from sole proprietor to employer, take a step back to confirm that hiring is part of your bigger business goal. What kind of company are you trying to build? What is your vision for your business? How large are you aiming to be in five years? In ten? Are employees necessary to make that happen? Are you sure? Most important, do you really want employees?

Granted, not having any supplemental help, whether consultants, contractors, interns, temps, or part-time or full-time workers, will, almost by definition, limit your growth. That's not necessarily bad. Not having employees does provide a level of flexibility and freedom that is appealing to many entrepreneurs. You can control the pace at which your business grows and can decide for yourself the maximum amount of work you want to take on at any given time. That doesn't mean that you won't need help from time to time. You can then ramp up or scale back as appropriate; it's fairly simple because you have only your salary and expenses to cover, that is, if you are taking a salary at this point (that's a topic for another time).

If you want to retain supplemental workers when you need them, and only when you need them, you can work through temporary staffing or consulting firms. For example, an accountant can serve a certain number of clients 10 months of the year, without the need for part- or full-time employees, and then hire supplemental workers around tax time. Such an arrangement enables the accountant to meet his or her business goals without saddling the firm with unnecessary labor costs during the majority of the year.

On the other hand, your clients' needs are also something to be considered. Can you continue to serve your clientele single-handedly? Are the clients satisfied with the current level of service you're giving them? Or are you stretching yourself a bit thin? Running a successful and growing business requires the careful balancing of your clients' needs and your financial needs, as well as your business vision.

Your business plan may include maintaining your solo business, with help when required, but if your clients are becoming less satisfied with your level of performance or accessibility, you may face a difficult choice: increase your work capacity by paying for some help or scale back your client list. Many entrepreneurs would prefer to outsource some of that work in order to keep all of their clients, which again brings us back to the need for outside labor.

TIMING IS EVERYTHING

My advice is to put off hiring employees as long as you possibly can without damaging your client relationships. That is, let your workload dictate when the time is right to pay for outside help. If you can get your work done in a timely fashion and meet the commitments you've made to your clients, maybe you don't really need to give up some of your income to others. Yes, you may be working long hours in order to accomplish this, but you are also keeping your expenses low and your profits higher.

However, if your workload has swelled to the point that you can no longer do all of the work yourself and yet you want to continue adding more clients and projects, start looking for help. Trying to manage everything yourself while your workload increases is a recipe for burnout and dissatisfied clients. Yes, you'll be minimizing your expenses, but you may also be risking the loss of clients, which also minimizes profits. Don't let that happen. When you reach the point of being overwhelmed with work and know that it is not temporary or seasonal, a problem every entrepreneur would like to have, it really *is* time to get some help.

"Help" does not necessarily mean hiring full-time employees, however. You have several options with respect to supplementing your own work capacity, including the following.

- *Consultants.* Sometimes what you really need is specific expertise and guidance from a specialist. You can typically negotiate either a per-hour rate or a flat fee for access to a consultant, depending on how much time you need from him or her. The business relationship can be one time, short-term, or ongoing. It's up to you. The only downside of engaging consultants is that their hourly rate can be significantly higher than that of a contract worker.
- *Independent contractor.* Like a lower-level consultant, in some respects, independent contractors can fill in where you need them but are generally hands-on workers rather than consultants who oversee and manage projects. You pay an hourly rate, and they take care of their taxes and benefits.
- *Contract employee.* Very popular in the corporate sector, contract employees are hired for a specific length of time, sometimes committed to a particular project or job, with no long-term employment commitment on your part. The advantage of contract employees is that when a project is completed, you have no ongoing financial commitment to them. However, the cost to tap into their skills is a bit higher than that of a full-time, permanent employee.

- *Temporary worker*. Retained through a staffing firm, "temp" workers can be a godsend if you've been overloaded by administrative tasks. Paid on an hourly basis, you can hire a temp—or several—to pitch in for a day, a week, or as needed. The hourly rate is higher than what you would pay a full-time assistant or secretary because of agency fees tacked on top of what the worker will be paid, but you have no further obligation when they walk out the door.

- *College or high school intern*. Many schools offer their students academic credit for a semester spent pitching in at a local business like yours. In exchange for earmarking specific tasks for the student to complete for you—more than just copying and filing—you may be able to land some free talent for a few months. Some internships are paid, however, so be clear about your pay limitations (if you have any) before you begin interviewing candidates.

- *Part-time worker*. If you're not ready to commit to a full-time employee but you know that your needs are permanent and ongoing, one option is to ease into a full-time arrangement with a part-time schedule at first. You can see how the worker fares and determine whether you have enough work to fill a 40-hour work week, too.

Determining which type of worker will be best for your business will depend on whether your need is temporary or permanent and what skill level you're after. The more expertise you need, such as the specialized information technology know-how our company required, the more you should expect to pay.

Revenue Generating or Not

Another factor in your hiring decision is whether the position you are filling represents a revenue-generating role. That is, will the person in that job be creating income for the company, such as through billable work or sales, or will he or she be non-revenue-generating, as is the case with executive staff and administrative personnel. Granted, all of those functions are needed for the company to succeed, but too many executives and too few income-producing workers can lead to trouble.

Before you hire any manager or executive who will be non-revenue-producing, first ask what value he or she can bring to the company. Just because some managers are not directly responsible for revenue generation does not mean that they can't play a role. For example, is the executive bringing existing client relationships to the table that could be beneficial to you as his or her employer? Or, even better, will he or she be bringing clients along when moving to your company? Or does he or she have ties to a particular contract, making it more likely that any bid from you will be more favorably received?

With any new employees, but especially with well-compensated executives and business development staff members, be sure to set goals and monitor how well they fill their new role with your business. Sure, they may look great on paper and have glowing references, but that doesn't mean that you shouldn't monitor their progress and work activity for the first few months. Many small-business owners assume that every new hire is doing what he or she is expected to do when sometimes that is definitely not the case.

To be sure that you don't get stuck with nonperforming or underperforming employees, frequently assess what all new employees are doing. I suggest a quarterly review of performance for the first six months, followed by an annual evaluation at minimum. Are they catching on? Is the client satisfied with their performance and work product? Are they contributing to the company's bottom line? Most small-business owners wait too long to evaluate a new employee's performance and are sometimes surprised to discover how little their great new hire is doing. If an employee is non-revenue-generating, make the decision to cut your losses sooner rather than later; three to six months is ample time to determine whether he or she is adding value to the company.

There are no hard-and-fast rules for how long it should take for an employee to catch on to his or her new job responsibilities, so you'll need to gauge for yourself whether your employee is contributing as much as you would like or need. Typically, a three- to six-month time frame is appropriate for management-level positions with broader responsibilities to get up to speed. They have to learn about the company's processes, procedures, products, services, clients, goals, and objectives, among other things. Technical and administrative skill sets acclimate slightly easier because of their specialization and portability of skills. Note that the more specialized the skills, the more you are paying and the more you have at stake.

THE GOING RATE

There are no absolutes when it comes to an appropriate salary, either. Each geographic area, industry, level of experience, and position has its own definition of what kind of benefits package is considered "competitive."

Back in the 1990s, when we were feverishly hiring IT professionals to support the government contracts we were starting to win, such skills were readily available in the Washington, D.C., area, and workers expected to be paid well. The National Association of Colleges and Employers reported that the starting-salary offers to computer science majors ranged from $45,000 to $58,000. So while we could have certainly offered applicants less than that, we knew that the further we went below the market rate, the fewer candidates we would attract.

Sometimes, however, paying more is just not possible. Perhaps the business simply does not have the cash flow to afford to compensate workers more. In our case, our salary offers were capped at times because we had government contracts that limited the size of the salaries we could afford to offer while still making a profit and providing competitive benefits. Most government contractors face this situation at one time or another because of the bid process. As part of preparing a proposal, or bid, on a government contract, you set the salaries to be paid the workers assigned to the task at hand, the overhead expenses, the general and administrative (G&A) costs, and the profit. The process can be tricky because you want to be competitive in your total bid in order to be able to afford the workers you know you'll need, but you don't want to go too high to knock your company out of competitive range.

In the case of business development staff members, the base salary you have to offer may be of less importance to potential hires than the commission offered on any new business they bring in. You can incentivize sales workers by offering a hefty percentage of the contract values they win for the company. Such arrangements keep your salary expenses low while encouraging employees to perform to their highest abilities.

Your geographic area also plays a role in determining the level of compensation that local employees are willing to accept. For example, in Washington, D.C., where government contractors are plentiful, the salaries for IT professionals are higher than in other areas. In other parts of the country, such as in major metropolitan areas, salaries are also higher. You'll want to take that into account as you start to budget for employees.

Online resources such as www.imercer.com, www.payscale.com, and www.salary.com may be helpful starting points to learn more about what you should expect to pay staff members based on their work experience and technical expertise. Professional and trade associations for your industry may also have salary survey data to share about what members are paying.

The salary or pay level you offer is really only part of the compensation equation: most employees today also expect some level of benefits. That includes a package containing some combination of health, dental, and vision insurance, life insurance of at least one times salary, a 401(k) plan with employer matching, tuition assistance, flexible work schedules, telecommuting, paid time off, end-of-year bonuses, etc. Without the ability to offer any benefits at all, attracting quality employees will be a bigger challenge.

When we started, we couldn't offer much, but we knew we needed to be able to offer at least basic benefits or we simply wouldn't have been competitive. Over time, as we grew, we were able to afford better and better benefits packages to offer our current and new employees.

At the most senior levels, some executives will ask for an ownership stake in your company or at least a path to ownership. That does not mean that you need to consider offering ownership, but it is certainly an enticement. You can also structure such a deal in ways to make it advantageous to everyone. For example, one of my key executive hires understood my resistance to relinquishing ownership. However, his goal was to make a certain salary, and he needed a secondary life insurance policy so that his family would be taken care of in the event that something happened to him. In this case, a policy referred to as "keyman insurance" was enough enticement. Therefore, we structured a deal whereby his salary could be achieved by meeting certain performance metrics and the keyman policy was an added bonus. Tying compensation to achieving results for the company kept him working harder, and it was a win-win for everyone.

Keep in mind that few companies grant ownership on day one, but you can make ownership an incentive to perform. Tie a stake in the company to the achievement of certain goals over time, for example, or accomplishment of a specific business objective. You can also require that the employee give back any shares in the company if he or she leaves within a certain period of time.

On the other hand, if a senior employee is willing to invest money up front in the company, you may also be more willing to grant—essentially, sell—a stake in the company in exchange. The decision is a personal one that business owners need to make for themselves on the basis of what they get in return for giving up a percentage of their business, which we addressed earlier in Chapter 3.

RECRUITING THE RIGHT TALENT

Sometimes finding the right talent to help grow your business can be challenging, especially in a tight job market or when you need very specialized skills, as we often did for government projects. Certainly, finding short-term workers was easier and could be met with contract help or temps, but for long-term projects, such as the five-year contracts we pursued, short-term arrangements wouldn't work. Employees who have experience working on government contracts know how the process works, so they come to expect full-time salaries and benefits.

Early on, we relied heavily on word of mouth and placing ads in the local newspapers. When all else failed, we turned to recruiting firms to find the talent we needed quickly. Having access to talented IT professionals was critical for our success, and we gladly paid recruiting fees in order to meet our hiring goals. At the time, we needed to prove our company's ability to perform on the IT contracts we had won, and recruiters simplified the process of finding the employees we needed.

As a small business, a relative newcomer, we also didn't have the time or human resources necessary to devote to doing our own recruiting initially. Retaining professionals for that reason made much more sense.

Once we started doing some of our own hiring, we used several outlets simultaneously to shorten the time required to find solid candidates. In addition to our own career page on the company Web site, we also used other outlets, including major career Web sites such as www.washingtonpost.com/jobs, www.monster.com, www.dice.com, and www.careerbuilder.com, where we publicized our hiring needs and gathered résumés. Many if not all of these sites charge a fee for posting positions; therefore, be sure to do your research carefully. For local hiring, you may also want to check local job search sites affiliated with your daily newspaper; in our case, that was the *Washington Post* and the *Baltimore Sun*.

Workers with certain backgrounds were already posting their résumés online in search of new opportunities. With access to the databases mentioned earlier, we found it easier to search for specific skills, experience, and technical or administrative backgrounds. A benefit of such sites is that they are reasonably up-to-date with current information on the potential prospects.

In addition to online sourcing, we also used offline sources such as the following.

- *Job fairs.* General gatherings designed to connect workers with available jobs
- *Trade shows.* Industry conferences and events where professionals network and update their skills
- *Industry days.* Targeted job fairs for people with very specific skills or certifications
- *Holding in-house job fairs.* Holding our own job fair brought candidates right to our doorstep
- *Professional associations.* Groups and organizations that consist of people with certain backgrounds or training with job banks you can tap into
- *Chambers of commerce.* Local chambers may also have a job bank or be willing to communicate your job openings to the business community
- *Business trade journals.* Industry-specific journals that are read by your targeted population

Our goal in using all of these sources was to create a steady stream of résumés and job applicants so we never had to invest too much time at the last minute searching for just the right professional for a particular contract we were pursuing or one we had recently won. Relying on several online and offline sources increased the diversity and quantity of job applicants from which we had to choose.

One of our best recruiting methods, however, was our employee referral program (ERP). This program encouraged our existing employees to assist us in recruiting the best-qualified individuals, by referring their colleagues and friends. We recognized that as we grew, identifying and recruiting qualified professionals would become an ever-increasing challenge. Therefore, we sought to reward the referring employees financially for being quasi-internal recruiters for the company. This move turned out to be the right motivation to get positions filled. For instance, when a current employee referred a qualified candidate to the company, he or she became eligible for a monetary incentive. If the referral was hired, performed successfully, and remained with the company for three months, the referring employee received a cash payment ranging from $500 for an administrative/clerical position to $2,000 for someone with specialized information technology experience. In fact, a couple of our employees were regular referral sources and supplemented their income by several thousands of dollars each year. I would say it was a win-win for everyone, really, and it was our most effective hiring tool.

Eventually, once our hiring needs became significant and ongoing, we hired our own internal recruiter to perform the function we had initially outsourced to our own employees. Yes, we now had another full-time employee on staff, but we were saving money on fees paid to the recruiting firms. With an employee of our own, we could provide additional incentives to help fill positions that were especially difficult.

Keep in mind that each staffing need should have its own position description. The description describes the duties of the position, education requirements, technical skills and certifications, if required, and any other qualifications that are relevant. Whether hiring a management member, a receptionist, or an engineer, we created a position description to help us evaluate each applicant. The position description became a key tool in the recruiting process, in a sense, and employees used it as a source for likely candidates. It became the criterion for our hiring decisions.

NOT ALL HIRES ARE WINNERS

Although you may be very clear about the skill set you need or the background you'd like a particular new hire to bring to the company, you'll eventually discover that some employees are much better on paper. Fortunately, we didn't make too many poor hiring choices, but there were a few. Surprisingly, it was never the candidates we were a little unsure of; in a couple of cases, we were downright shocked by who the poor performers turned out to be.

One memorable employee was a senior executive whom we felt fortunate to have found and hired away from a major company. It was a coup, we felt, to have wooed him away from his former employer.

His track record was excellent, his references were stellar, and he had a background as a proven producer, making us certain he would make significant contributions to the company.

Because he was used to having certain resources at his disposal, I spent a fair amount of time discussing with him during the interviews the fact that everyone at RGII was very hands-on; he would need to do almost all of his administrative work himself. He seemed excited by the challenge.

So imagine my surprise when, during his first few weeks on the job, he requested his own assistant. Uh, no, even our senior executives don't have assistants, I explained. He didn't get it.

When we hired him, we set very specific goals up front for his performance. He was sure that he would have no trouble at all meeting them. In fact, he expected to quickly exceed them, he told us, by bringing in some contracts almost immediately. Sadly, after six months, he had not delivered on any of his promises or goals and seemed to be nowhere near accomplishing any of them, even within a 12-month window. We had to let him go.

Other poor hires were simply lacking in common sense, such as the worker who used his corporate American Express card to pay for personal services or the nudist employee who enjoyed running around in the park at night.

That's why investing a fair amount of time up front is important; carefully screen, interview, check references, and run background checks on every potential new hire, if possible. You might say that those are just more expenses you can't afford. You're right, but in the long run, you may save additional recruitment costs. Even social-networking Web sites such as LinkedIn, MySpace, and Facebook are now resources you can leverage to learn more about job candidates before you make an offer. You need to feel confident that they will represent you in a professional and positive manner at all times. During Monday morning orientations, I would tell new employees, "Our reputation is on the line every day we open our doors. Therefore, your behavior is a direct reflection of who we are as a company. Let's make a good impression."

DO FAMILY AND FRIENDS MAKE GOOD EMPLOYEES?

Let's face it; early on in your small-business career, you may not be able to afford the luxury of turning down free help that is offered by people who care about you. Your mother offers to come in and act as a receptionist in a pinch or your best friend promises to do some Internet research you need to do but haven't yet had a chance to get to. Are you really going to say "no"?

Some entrepreneurs would caution you about accepting help from friends and family because of the trouble it can lead to later on if the employee/employer relationship doesn't work out. True, there are pitfalls, but many small businesses wouldn't be where they are today without the volunteer help of their inner circle.

When we had the opportunity to hire friends and family, we took it, and most of the time, everything worked out well. My niece is one example of an employee who was an excellent addition to the company. Almost always, when we hired family and friends, we ended up with good employees we could trust and who were committed to our success. But once in a while, difficult situations did arise, such as the time Greg had to fire his brother. Yes, his brother. Some misunderstandings arose about the level of performance we expected, and ultimately, the pairing just didn't work out. The relationship, however, did survive.

Even more dangerous than an underperforming family member, however, is the perception that other employees have of those people and of you, the owner. Some may resent those closest to you, perceiving that they don't have to work as long, as hard, or as adeptly as everyone else. Granted, that perception may be false, but it can still have a disastrous impact on employee morale.

To avoid misunderstanding and misperception, make it clear to everyone—but especially those close to you—what your expectations are. Make sure that they understand that they will be given no special treatment. Once that's out of the way, you may truly enjoy having your relatives and friends working with you.

EMPLOYEE RETENTION: KEEPING THEM ONCE YOU'VE HIRED THEM

Of course, after investing a significant amount of time and effort to identify and attract top employees, your next challenge as a business owner is holding on to them. Because top performers are routinely offered enticements to jump ship, you need to take steps to make your company an attractive employer. To fend off the advances other companies may be making, you first need to be sure that the compensation package and work environment you're offering are at least competitive, if not above average. The more above average you are, the less apt your employees may be to leave.

Some of the factors employees evaluate when deciding whether to stay with or leave an employer include the following:

- Challenging work environment
- Competitive salaries
- Comprehensive benefits package
- Opportunities for career growth and advancement
- Performance incentive programs, better known as bonuses
- Telecommuting opportunities
- Flexible work schedule
- Corporate culture
- Longevity of assignments
- Professional development opportunities
- Education and training availability
- Feeling they are valued and not just a random employee
- Recognition for their contribution to the company
- Direct management contact

The more you can offer from this list, the better your odds are of being able to woo capable employees away from other businesses and then keep them.

Another piece of the retention puzzle is employee morale, which you can try to impact but over which you really have little control. Some of the steps we took at RGII to develop a sense of camaraderie and teamwork were semiannual events, including an employee picnic in the summer, a holiday party at the end of the year, pizza days that the division managers would host every once in a while for their teams, as well as premiums, such as polo/golf shirts, mugs, mouse pads, and umbrellas with the company logo on them, to help foster pride in their workplace. In addition, we recognized employees formally with individual and team awards and informally with on-the-spot bonus awards. This type of recognition served as motivation for employees to increase their creativity and productivity.

Although you will lose employees for various reasons, for us it was mostly correlated with the completion or loss of a contract. Unfortunately, that's just part of the process. That being said, we were fortunate to have a very high retention rate, which we attributed to valuing our greatest asset, the employees themselves.

For those employees who did leave, we always scheduled an exit interview to better understand why they were going elsewhere and what, if anything, we could have done to make the employment experience more rewarding. If we discovered something we could control, we made changes to minimize the chance of other employees also leaving. Through exit interviews, we also identified potentially disgruntled employees who might later try to take some legal action against us; these were usually the employees who refused to participate in the exit interview. Recognizing that court actions would take time and energy away from our goal of growing the company, we did our very best to promote a positive work environment and keep our talented employees satisfied.

We recognized that our employees truly were the company's greatest asset. Without them, we could never have been as successful as we were, and we tried to make sure that they knew that not only by telling them as often as possible how much we appreciated their contributions but also by rewarding them.

LESSONS LEARNED

If hiring employees is part of the business plan, remember that they are the company's greatest asset. Don't forget to thank them often for a job well done.

☑ Whether employees make sense for your business depends on your long-term business plan. Do you aspire to create a large company that grows beyond your personal capabilities? Or are you more interested in controlling your schedule and your workload, in creating a job for yourself and supporting your lifestyle? Employees may not make sense for every organization; it all depends on the type of company you want to have.

☑ To keep expenses low and profits higher, wait patiently and decide wisely before hiring your employees. Do as much as you can yourself for as long as possible. When you reach a point where product or service quality may suffer, you know that you need to bring in reinforcements.

☑ When you can, hire more revenue-generating workers than non-revenue-generating to help ensure that your overhead costs don't skyrocket beyond your incoming revenue.

☑ Don't rush into making a long-term, permanent employment commitment. There are several ways of obtaining help without going the full-time route. You can bring in a consultant to help you strategize, problem solve, or address specific needs. Hiring part-time, contract, or temp workers as needed will also reduce expenses.

☑ Before offering any kind of pay range, use online tools to determine what the going rate is for your geographic region, industry, and skill level.

(continued on page 96)

LESSONS LEARNED
(continued from page 95)

☑ Investigate what kind of benefits you can offer your workers. Even if your compensation package consists solely of a salary and health insurance, that may be enough to entice employees to join a growing company. Benefits such as flex time and telecommuting may also be highly valued, and they cost you next to nothing to offer. Over time, try to add more benefits, such as tuition assistance, a 401(k) plan, dental and vision insurance, and whatever else your employees value.

☑ Offering an ownership stake in the company to any employee must come with conditions, such as making an investment in the business or receiving the ownership opportunity only upon achieving specified performance objectives, such as a certain revenue level or profit margin.

☑ To find top employees, use your Web site to post job openings and other major Web sites to announce available openings and do some active sourcing. Evaluate résumés posted on job sites and in professional association databases. Attend job fairs, trade shows, and even host your own to identify potential candidates. One of the best strategies, however, is to offer your current employees financial incentives to recommend other talented professionals who are their friends and colleagues.

☑ Retaining employees requires more than merely offering a paycheck. You should also aim to provide a challenging work environment and opportunities for growth and advancement. In addition, remember to communicate how valued each and every worker is to your company's success; feeling appreciated can go a long way in retaining your best workers.

CHAPTER 6

DETERMINING YOUR COMPETITIVE ADVANTAGES

"Everyone who competes in the games goes into strict training. They do it to get a crown that will not last; but we do it to get a crown that will last forever." — 1 Corinthians 9:25

When I first started RGII, my company's competitive advantage was me—everything I knew and had experienced and could leverage to aid my business. Back then, in the beginning, I *was* the business. Until I hired employees, consultants, and advisors, my company's strengths and weaknesses mirrored my own.

Early on in the life of most, if not all, small businesses, the company's true competitive advantage is you: your skills, personal experiences, reputation, background, and network of contacts. Whatever proficiencies and knowledge you have provide the foundation for your company's competitive position. When your company consists of you and only you, whatever makes you stand out is what will make your business succeed.

Later, when you have other people involved, your business's advantages, also referred to as competitive discriminators, will expand to include the skills, abilities, and personal relationships of those who support your company. That is your first source for obtaining competitive advantage: the internal skills, abilities, intellectual capital, capabilities, and expertise you and your business possess.

Your second source of competitive advantage is an in-depth knowledge of your clients' missions and those innovative solutions that demanding clients require. The more knowledge, the greater the competitive advantage. The presence of both depth and breadth of client knowledge is a key ingredient, albeit not in its entirety, to long-term client loyalty. The objective with this level of knowledge is persuading the clients that your company is the sole possessor of the product or service solution they need. In this case, the knowledge discriminator becomes almost bulletproof.

A company's know-how and a comprehensive knowledge base of how your clients do business are two critical differentiators that can set your company apart and shelter, but not totally impede, the competition from your clients' domain. That is the true power of competitive advantages.

YOUR CURRENT COMPETITIVE ADVANTAGES

What exactly are your competitive advantages? What separates or distinguishes your company from the competition?

Your competitive advantages are both the tangible and the intangible attributes of the company that are superior and that differentiate you from the competition, in the hopes of influencing a client's buying decision in a positive way while shifting attention away from the competition. You can be different from the competition by charging sky-high prices, but that is not a differentiator that will attract hoards of new clients. However, your willingness to be available to clients on a moment's notice most certainly is an advantage on which your clients will come to rely.

Your business probably has at least one competitive advantage already, but you need to identify all of the advantages so you can effectively articulate those benefits to current and potential clients. Start by examining what strengths you currently possess. Your strengths are those elements of your business that give you an advantage over other businesses, what your clients would view as positive must-haves for the organization.

To determine what strengths you, the business owner, have that could be leveraged as competitive indicators, ask yourself the following questions.

- *What do I know?* What skills have I gained? What experiences have I had? What industries have I worked in? What specialized knowledge have I amassed? What other information do I have access to that gives me a leg up over the competition?
- *Where have I been?* What companies have I worked for? What countries have I lived in? What job assignments have I had that give me an outlook different from that of my competition?
- *Who do I know?* Who do I have access to by virtue of the high school I went to, the college I graduated from, the associations I belong to, the business associations I have developed during my

career, the church or temple I attend, or the family members I have with ties to decision makers with whom I want to do business?

■ *How am I different from other business owners?* What are my priorities, ambitions, and goals for my business and me?

■ *Why have I succeeded thus far?* What habits, or approach to business, do I have that are different from those around me?

For some small businesses, the strengths of the owner are all the company has. However, if you already have other workers or partners, you'll want to conduct the same fact-finding mission with them as well. Ask the same questions of your team: what specialized or inside knowledge do they have that others may not? What kind of track record can they claim? What personal relationships do they have that could be a stepping stone to a lucrative client opportunity? You may even want to go so far as to have employees complete a skills inventory to identify their unique talents up front. As you hire new employees, evaluate the skill sets and experiences those employees bring to your business. With each new staff member, your strengths, opportunities, and competitive position shift and grow.

Each new employee certainly brings new skills to the company, but over time, your business itself also develops its own corporate track record, which is separate and distinct from the individual employees that compose the business. That past performance history, which documents the company's ability to successfully complete client projects, also enhances the company's competitive position. The more clients you have and the more projects you complete on time, within budget, and with innovation, the stronger your track record becomes. A strong record gives potential clients the confidence that you can perform just as well or better for them.

A growing client list also benefits your company in ways that go beyond additional revenue and credibility. Each client project, assignment, or client transaction brings with it additional knowledge and information that can then be applied to future projects. For example, creating a tool kit for your alpha client and then transferring new knowledge, best practices, and high-caliber subject matter experts to other clients significantly enhance your value proposition. With this knowledge transfer come substantial cost savings and quality improvements that are delivered directly to the clients. As a result, other competitive advantages and discriminators will emerge.

COMPETITIVE DISCRIMINATORS

In addition to the advantages derived from owners and employees, small businesses can develop competitive discriminators by virtue of their size. Some of those benefits that clients may enjoy and perceive as advantages include the following.

Responsiveness. Smaller businesses, with fewer layers of management and administration, can often respond more quickly to client requests than can their larger corporate brethren. With less bureaucracy come direct access to senior managers and a faster turnaround on work that needs to occur.

Speed. Similarly, smaller companies can react more quickly to just about any situation.

Speed in particular is one advantage small-business owners should leverage as much as possible, because in my opinion larger competitors may outspend and grow faster, but small businesses can keep a steady pace and be responsive to clients. For example, several years ago, RGII won a contract to establish a call center in Oklahoma to support the U.S. Housing and Urban Development (HUD) agency. One of the contract requirements was to have the call center fully operational and manned with trained staff within 30 days. Despite the fact that we were headquartered in Maryland, 1,300 miles away, we knew that we could meet the terms of the contract by reallocating and deploying the right resources with the speed of companies with a much larger presence.

Our deployment operations entailed human resource personnel, coupled with operations staff members, who immediately flew to the client site in Oklahoma to size up our task. Within three weeks—one whole week before the deadline—we had successfully leased office space and had acquired, recruited, hired, and trained employees for all the key positions.

Without paperwork and bureaucracy of a larger organization to slow the process or a chain of command that needs to approve each decision, smaller businesses can get to work almost immediately on behalf of a client.

Lower costs. In many cases, the lower overhead that small businesses may enjoy is passed along to clients in the form of lower prices. As long as the end user, the client, is confident that the company has the resources necessary to complete the work or successfully fulfill the terms of a contract, lower costs can be a powerful advantage.

Flying under the radar. Because of their size, small businesses are frequently underestimated by their competition. But being overlooked can prove to be an advantage to small businesses, which are less likely to have their weaknesses highlighted by competitors during the sales process. They are not perceived to be a threat, so their competitors are less likely to "sell against them," pointing out how and why their product or service is superior to potential clients.

Expertise. While larger companies have sizable business development and research and development (R&D) budgets, smaller companies in the process of developing products or software-related technologies often invest a significant percentage of revenues in R&D, yielding more innovation relatively quickly. On the other hand, smaller service companies without a development-type offering invest their resources in the development of expertise through intellectual capital, their people, in order to create the solutions their clients need to achieve their missions. By doing so, companies quickly earn a positive reputation for delivering expertise where it's needed the most, within the four walls of client organizations.

Location. From the clients' perspective, proximity to their offices can be a major competitive advantage. Small businesses located only a few miles away are often perceived to be more accessible and better able to service the needs of their clients than companies situated hundreds or thousands of miles away.

Knowledge of Your Clients

In addition to knowing what internal resources you have to leverage or build on, you also should assess how well you know your clients, because that, too, can be a significant competitive discriminator.

Ideally, you should know each of your clients—regardless of size—inside and out. In fact, knowledge of a client requires comprehensive intelligence gathering before proposing to do business with a prospective client. This extra effort provides a major advantage over other companies competing for the organization's business.

Some of the key pieces of intelligence you should gather early on about each client, present or potential, include the following.

- *What does the organization do?* This seems basic, but too few businesses take the time to figure out what business their potential client is in. What does it sell or provide? Who are its target markets? Is it B2B or B2C? Who are its suppliers? Who is its parent company or agency, if it has one? This can shape the resources it has access to and its future direction.
- *What is the organization's mission?* Why does it exist? What is its purpose? How does it serve its constituents? What does success look like for this client? Once you know that, you can better position your company to support its success.
- *What industry is the organization in?* Again, this may seem basic, but knowing whether your future client is in technology, education, or government, for example, will impact how you position your company as a potential business partner. How large is the industry? Who are the leaders?

What are some of the industry trends that are occurring and affecting the client?

■ *Who are all the players within the organization?* Who is your point of contact? What is the chain of command? Who are the decision makers? Understanding the players, their reporting relationships, and their specific challenges and concerns will assist you in developing a client-specific strategy aimed at creating a competitive advantage.

■ *What trends or major changes are occurring?* With change comes opportunity. Therefore, be watchful for technological or legislative shifts that could impact the company's ability to service clients. Such forethought better positions the company to propose additional products and/or services in anticipation of such changes.

To gather details about a potential client, some of the best sources to start with include the following.

■ *The organization's own Web site.* Nearly every government agency, corporation, educational institution, and nonprofit has its own Web site, where visitors can learn about the organization; its mission, structure, and management team; who is serviced; core products and services; and much more.

■ *A printed information packet, media kit, or annual report* (also available from corporate clients). Most corporations do significant subcontract work with small businesses as part of their supplier diversity programs, especially those that are women-owned and/or minority enterprises. Whether number one on the Fortune 500 list (Wal-Mart) or number 500 (SCANA Corporation), registering to become a potential supplier to these organizations is as easy as visiting their Web site and downloading the appropriate application.

■ *Google.com.* For a basic rundown of recent and past headlines about the organization and links to articles that may quote your point of contact or cite particular issues the organization is facing, do a Google search. Keep in mind once again that the Internet did not get a public face until the 1990s and Google. com did not come into existence until 1996. So, the technology available to us today was not available when I first started RGII. Therefore, the gathering of intelligence and other information pertaining to a potential client target required more legwork, literally.

When we were developing the business plan for RGII, we met with the small-business office at targeted federal agencies to gather information on which small businesses were currently doing business there. The small-business advocates were generally very helpful, considering that their mission is to ensure that small businesses are treated fairly and have an opportunity not only to compete but also to receive an equitable share of the agency's contracting and subcontracting dollars. We also relied on the small-business office to give us information on who the buyers were within the agencies (which goes back to obtaining copies of an agency forecast, as I spoke of earlier) and what companies were currently doing business with them and in which areas. That information helped us identify who our competitors were for various types of contracts and, in some cases, confirmed an opportunity within the agency we might not have known about otherwise. Determining who your competitors are in order to maintain a competitive advantage must not be overlooked or taken lightly.

KNOWLEDGE OF THE COMPETITION

Knowing who your competitors are can shape how you market your business as you stretch to show your competitive discriminators—but be realistic in your information gathering. You cannot know everything about every competitor. It is not necessary, nor is it a good use of your time to even try. Instead, focus on your top 10 competitors at first. Then, over time, as your company grows, you can narrow that list to your top five competitors.

Your list of competitors will also shift over time. As you carve out your own product, solution, and/or service niche, some competitors will fade away, and others will appear. With the invention of the Internet, information is readily available on the competition, such as identity, location, service and product offerings, customers, contracts, recent news, job opportunities—the list goes on. Vetting the wealth of information on your competitors and then utilizing it to best position your company to compete against them and/or partner with them helps to create key strategic advantages, such as innovation and new product development, best practices, and possible process improvement opportunities. Understanding the competition and formulating a strategy to compete actually provides the client with another viable choice to bring about change and resolve problems within the organization.

Finding out who the competition is requires research and assessment. Research not only competing products and services but also the position of the competition within the market and its core strengths and weaknesses. Some of this information is not readily available. A competitor's weakness, for example, won't be immediately known; however, as you begin to gain presence in a particular market, the world suddenly becomes smaller, and that information becomes a conversation piece.

Other sources include the following.

- *Industry newspapers and trade magazines.* Within the federal government market, we were avid readers of *Washington Technology*. Published bimonthly, it is the only national newspaper that delivers essential business news to business executives whose companies provide high-level technical services to the government. Each issue features the latest contracting wins, government initiatives and projects, case studies and analyses, and fresh technology news. Not only does the publication report important news within the industry but also it produces the *Washington Technology* Fast 50, a listing that recognizes some of the most successful small businesses in the government market that have experienced phenomenal growth over the past five years. This list that represented our competition became an invaluable source of competitive information.

- In addition to *Washington Technology*, we also frequently referred to *Federal Computer Week* and *Government Computer News* for the latest information on government IT initiatives. For competitors outside of the government, *Inc.* magazine also publishes news about the fastest-growing small businesses nationwide. Regardless of your industry, you are more than likely to find a similar "top something" list from which you can begin to identify key competitors for your products and/or services.

- *Trade shows.* Don't feel that you need to exhibit at major trade shows; participating as an attendee can be just as valuable. You can get as much, and maybe more, information simply by walking the floors and chatting with exhibitors. The key trade shows we attended as both an exhibitor and an attendee included FOSE, an IT event known government-wide and the annual meeting place for the industry (www.fose.com). This event brings together more than 10,000 senior-level IT decision makers from federal, state, local, and international government converging in one location in Washington, D.C., to learn, network, share experiences, and evaluate products, services, and solutions from more than 400 industry partners.

By attending events of this nature, you come face to face with the top competitors in your market and get to see firsthand, up close and in person, what they are selling to potential clients. It becomes a great networking opportunity as well.

Using Information to Your Advantage

If this information-gathering process sounds time-consuming, it is. Learning about potential clients up front takes time, but it will also help separate you from your competition. By studying your prospects in advance of any written proposal or oral presentation, you will significantly increase your odds of impressing your prospect and positioning your company for winning new business.

We found that most companies went into bid presentations prepared to talk almost entirely about their company, their capabilities, and their successes. Very little about the government agency was ever addressed; it was all about them.

This was great for RGII because in every bid we submitted to potential clients, we tried to demonstrate that we understood their mission and challenges and sought to bring problem resolution and innovative solutions. We revealed the research we had done and the problems and challenges we knew about and then made product and service recommendations that specifically addressed the issues we knew they were facing. We never submitted a generic, one-size-fits-all solution; each had to be tailor-made for every client. A comprehensive approach and innovative solutions, trisected with client knowledge, were instrumental in assisting our clients in making an informed decision when selecting us as their contractor of choice. Intelligence gathering and compiling background information were certainly part of RGII's competitive advantage in bidding on government contracts.

On the back end of each bid process, we also requested a "debriefing," which is government speak for an explanation of what we did well and areas where we could have addressed the needs of the client better. Whether we won or lost, we contacted the contracting officer at the agency issuing the contract and asked what made us stand out from the competition or what caused us not to be selected. These short briefs could be given either verbally or in writing, but regardless of the medium, the information received was invaluable feedback for the team. Understanding the competitive advantages and, in the case of a loss, the perceived weaknesses from the clients' perspective helped us build on the advantages and correct any deficiencies so we were better prepared for subsequent business opportunities. We used the debriefing to develop lessons learned, being careful to reuse effective and cost-efficient best practices and approaches while also retooling those areas that were deemed lacking by the client.

Retaining an Advantage

Once you discover your competitive advantages or develop them, you'll want to do all you can to maintain them. Don't give up that lead easily. To do that, do the following.

- Leverage what you are good at. Stay focused on strengthening your position as a product and/or service provider.
- Reinforce the positive image you and your company have earned. Success breeds success, and organizations prefer to do business with successful companies.
- Make sure your clients know what you are good at. They may have hired you for one area of expertise when your strong suit, your sweet spot, is actually something else entirely. Communicate that.
- Continue to reinforce and hone your competitive advantages. Once your competition sees you making a move into their territory, they will raise the bar. Be ready to outpace the competition and do more than just keep up with them; otherwise, you will surely be left behind.

Every company's competitive advantages will evolve. At the start, RGII's competitive advantages included the work experience Greg and I had, the relationships we had established with contracting officers, our knowledge of the government contracting marketplace, our professional reputations, and our education.

Within a few years, however, that list of advantages had changed dramatically, thanks to our growing employee ranks and the multitude of successful contracts. By the time RGII was at the multimillion-dollar mark in revenue, our advantages/discriminators included our diverse client base, the strategic alliances we had forged with larger companies, our extensive technical capabilities, innovativeness, responsiveness, productivity and effectiveness, a strong reputation in the industry, our solid leadership and ever-visible management team, and an identity based on integrity and quality of service. In addition to those competitive indicators, we were in a strong financial position by that point, which was one advantage—if not the biggest of them all. We were stable with impeccable credit, which made obtaining capital a cinch when we needed it to support the multimillion-dollar contracts that we were winning.

On the flip side, our weaknesses, or critical needs, also evolved. In the beginning, if you recall, we had little to no relationships with banks and no performance history to leverage, making financing almost impossible. We also understood how the Department of Defense procurement process worked, a plus, but we were not familiar with the preferences of civilian agencies, with which we were also pursuing new business. The company had a relatively short performance history, and our entire business development team consisted of Greg, which put us at a disadvantage against competitors with entire business development departments dedicated to quickly unearthing new contract opportunities.

By the time RGII was approaching $48 million in revenue, we had reached a peak in terms of critical needs. At that point, we had identified no less than 17 critical needs the company had to address. The difference between weaknesses and critical needs, as we saw it, was that weaknesses had no perceived solution; they were a disadvantage, pure and simple. Critical needs, on the other hand, consisted of a statement of the problem, why it was important to address, and what we recognized we needed to do about it.

For example, one such critical need was a full-time sales team. The fact that Greg, along with one or two other business developers, made up our sales team created a growth problem. We needed that to change in order for the company to continue growing, and the solution was to allocate a larger percentage of the budget to sales and marketing.

Sometimes, taking a step back from your company to view it as others do can also help pinpoint strengths and weaknesses. Ask yourself how you want others to perceive your company. Seek to measure and understand the competitive forces in your market and what would be needed to help you stand shoulders above and separate and distinct from the competition. Size up your competitors in their abilities and capabilities and then leverage your discriminators to outpace them within the marketplace. Easier said than done, you might say—and you are correct—but the measure of real success comes by doing and not just watching. Answering these kinds of questions can help you see your business as it is today and help you envision its long-term future.

LESSONS LEARNED

A company's competitive advantages are developed over time; however, the foundation of competitiveness is inherent in the intellect of the people and then transferred to the end user of that knowledge, the client.

☑ When assessing your company's competitive advantages or potential sources of advantage, start with you, the owner. What skills, abilities, background, experiences, and connections do you have that can be leveraged to benefit your company?

☑ In addition to your own skills and abilities, or those of your team members, your inside knowledge of your clients is another major competitive advantage. Even if you operate exactly like your closest competitor, if you know your clients better and have a stronger working relationship, you have the upper hand.

☑ Don't try to study or monitor every single one of your competitors; you'll waste too much time and overwhelm yourself with data. Instead, identify the top 10 competitors you seem to come up against routinely and research them. Over time, as your business grows and you narrow your focus, scale back and pay attention to your five major competitors.

(continued on page 113)

Lessons Learned
(continued from page 112)

☑ To learn as much as you can about the companies that are competing against you for the same clients, turn to sources such as the company's own Web site, the small-business office at government agencies, the SBA, professional associations, industry reports and Top 100 lists, Google.com, and other Web sites.

☑ Once you obtain a competitive advantage, it takes diligence and perseverance to maintain it, so don't lose it.

☑ Do all you can to continue to broaden your knowledge base and skill set, communicate positive news about your company that reinforces your image as successful, and convey to your clients all the products and services that you offer. In turn, you will create opportunities to broaden your range of support.

CHAPTER 7

MARKETING

"People can get many good things by the words they say; the work of their hands also gives them many benefits."
— *Proverbs 12:14*

In the beginning, we did not have a marketing budget. With the little capital we had to invest, we invested in traditional marketing materials, such as business cards and trifold brochures, and we reached out to our network of contacts in ways that did not require a large financial investment. We made phone calls and set up meetings to discuss our capabilities, conducted briefings, and gave tabletop presentations. Building on the relationships we had already established through our previous careers and the relationships we wanted to forge, we used the resources we had readily available for marketing, namely, our time, the phone, and our presence, to connect with those clients with whom we desired to do business. This was marketing in its purest form.

Making phone calls and scheduling meetings are part of a strategy that works, especially if the company is strong in experience and capability but lacking in capital to invest. In fact, personally connecting with a target client remains the best marketing tactic you can use, regardless of in which growth cycle the company happens to be. For a marketing strategy to be successful, a certain amount of legwork has to be done up front. Whether you are selling to the government, the corporate market, or consumers, there are marketing methods that work for all.

As with everything I have touched on throughout this book, marketing starts with planning—planning for which marketing methods will yield the results sought. Let's take a look at a few marketing strategies that have a high probability of generating results without breaking the bank. Although this list is not intended to be all inclusive, the following are some of the methods that small businesses frequently use.

MARKETING ALONG THE WAY

Jay Conrad Levinson, known as "the Father of Guerrilla Marketing," coined the term "guerrilla marketing" years ago in reference to innovative marketing and promotion tactics that business owners can use to spend less, accomplish more, and achieve substantial profits. Isn't that ultimately what business owners want to do? Absolutely.

The basic idea behind guerrilla marketing involves taking traditional marketing methods such as advertising, public relations, trade show participation, collateral materials, and telemarketing, to name a few, and finding ways to apply them at a fraction of the typical cost. While major corporations and well-funded nonprofits have marketing budgets that permit investments in many of these activities, small businesses typically have more limited funding. They also have to generate results from each marketing initiative. Unlike bigger organizations that can afford image/branding campaigns, smaller companies can't afford marketing that doesn't yield a significant and immediate return on that investment.

For us, the marketing methods that yielded the best return on our investment included the following.

Collateral material. Yes, you can spend a lot of money on brochures and leave-behinds (information about the company you leave with a potential prospect), but you don't need to spend more if you don't have to. Start-ups can design and produce a bare-bones but effective brochure for very little money. I know this because that is exactly what we did.

As we began making appointments with government officials to discuss RGII's capabilities and upcoming contracts, we found that bringing along printed materials that explained our services, capabilities, background, and performance history was important. Without some kind of brochure, I don't believe we would have been taken seriously. Yet, as you know, we did not have money set aside for this. Fortunately, we had a computer and a printer, and that's all we needed to design and print a simple brochure.

Granted, our first-generation trifold brochure was perhaps not as extravagant as our competitors', but it did the job. Just as our Power-Point presentation may not have been flashy, it cost us no extra money to prepare and present because the software came bundled with our computer.

To this day, I feel strongly that every small business selling to other businesses (B2B) should have printed collateral materials. A simple but professional-looking brochure or one-page summary is an important reference tool that helps prospects understand who you are, what you offer, and how what you do can possibly help them. The prospect has to be able to take you seriously as a business owner.

Web site creation. Although the Internet was in its infancy around the same time RGII Technologies was a start-up, today, regardless of size, companies must have a Web site. There is no question that an online presence with market-focused information is critical to success. In fact, it is expected.

Because the Web site is the most important marketing tool for getting the message out about your company to a large audience, it is imperative not only that the Web site be professional looking but also that it contain solid client-centric content. Think of it as an online capabilities brochure that can connect you with your target market at the touch of a button. Do you currently have a Web site? If not, get one. If you currently have one, does it reflect the best your company has to offer? Does it provide a visitor to the site background information about the company, its products and services, contact information, testimonials from satisfied clients, what clients are currently being serviced, etc.? All of this information is critical for an effective site. If you can't answer a strong "yes" to these questions, you should consider overhauling your existing online image. It is likely costing you in more ways than one.

While a Web site is perhaps the most important marketing tool, it can also be the most expensive. Nonetheless, you must have one. It simply isn't optional.

If your budget looks like ours did early on, you may be interested in some tips for creating a Web site for less. These include the following.

- Approach the chairperson of the graphic design department at a local college or university and ask whether he or she might like a class project to assign—of designing a Web site for you.
- If you don't want to wait several weeks for a class to design a site, you might also ask for referrals to talented students who might be interested in designing your Web site on the side for you.

- Sites such as www.elance.com and www.rentacoder.com are known as good places to find lower-cost talent, including Web site designers and copywriters.
- If you have the interest or aptitude, you might consider trying to set a site up yourself by using a free or low-cost Web design template. Search Google for "Web site templates" to find one that matches your vision for your site.
- For the content, try drafting it yourself and paying an editor to spiff it up later, which is less expensive than hiring someone to write it from scratch.

Once your Web site is up and running, be sure to update it as often as possible. No one likes to see a static site that hasn't been updated in years; that suggests that the company behind the site is less interested in remaining current and keeping clients or prospective clients up to date on the progress of the company. Keeping the information current and updating it often notifies search engines such as Google and moves your site higher in the search rankings.

As the company grows, the Web site can be as fancy and as interactive as your budget will allow. However, maintaining the primary functions of information accessibility, reliability, and timeliness will remain the key factors of an effective site regardless of how flashy it is.

E-mail communiqués. In the past decade, business use of telemarketing as a marketing tool has been eclipsed by the use of e-mail. Today, instead of picking up the telephone, more small businesses use e-mail to make introductions, forge connections, and share information. Its ease of use, convenience, popularity, and cost (free!) have pushed e-mail to the fore. But while e-mail is now the preferred means of communication for many, marketing via e-mail is still relatively new and can be viewed as impersonal.

Despite the recent trend toward e-mail communication, it should not replace the traditional phone call to connect with potential clients.

However, if email is your preferred communication method, one quick and easy way to establish an e-mail relationship with your clients is to invite them to sign up for important news from your company, delivered via e-mail. If you have your clients' e-mail addresses, you can send them a personalized message explaining your intent to communicate via e-mail and asking for their permission to do so. When they respond in the affirmative, you now have their OK to stay in touch.

Soon after you begin collecting client e-mail addresses, you will want to begin fulfilling your promise to provide relevant information. For many companies, that means creating an e-mail newsletter or bulletin that is distributed to your growing e-mail list on a regular basis.

Use e-mail the same way you would use direct mail: to communicate directly with your target audience and/or your clients—but at a small fraction of the cost of direct mail.

Direct mail. Because I've already brought up direct mail, I'll address it here by saying that few small businesses have the budget to afford to design, print, and mail much in the way of marketing materials. For us, direct mail came later, when RGII had a steady stream of both revenue and profits. At a minimum, one traditional direct mailing will cost several hundreds or thousands of dollars. Because many smaller companies, especially those in the start-up phase, either do not have an annual marketing budget or have a budget that is less than the cost of one campaign, I do not recommend that direct mail be at the top of your list of marketing tactics.

That said, there are a few ways to significantly reduce the cost of a direct-mail campaign. Reducing the design cost can make direct mail affordable; reducing the production cost is another option. Postage is the final cost element. Although the size and format of what you're designing will drive how much it costs to print or copy, most designers will agree that a postcard campaign is among the cheapest. That is true in part because postcards themselves are small but also because the cost to mail them through the U.S. Postal Service is also minimal, currently $.27 for first class and even less when sent bulk mail.

Where major corporations are still producing full-color, multipage mailers costing hundreds of thousands of dollars, savvy small-business owners know that they don't need to spend that kind of money to generate results from a direct-mail campaign. But with the swing toward e-mail that has occurred recently, companies looking to stand out need to invest in only a little traditional direct mail to make an impact.

Trade shows. Attending trade shows was a more effective marketing strategy for us than was direct mail. They were important because they helped us achieve our goal of getting in front of multiple government buyers at once. Whether we participated as show attendees, meaning that we roamed the aisles introducing ourselves to government agencies that were exhibiting, or we, ourselves, were exhibitors, distributing materials about the company and making short, on-the-spot presentations to purchasing agents who were checking out exhibitors, we found trade shows to be an excellent use of our time. Where else could we introduce ourselves and meet with multiple government contracting officers in one place?

The best part was that many of the trade shows, especially the industry shows, were free, which was right in line with our marketing budget. As the company grew in size, we were able to invest in a tabletop display, followed by a professionally designed portable floor-sized panel system that did a better job of presenting RGII not only to potential prospects but also to our competition. We were able to use these systems over and over again, and we kept costs down by having our in-house designer design the display panels specifically for the trade show we were attending.

A bigger consideration was how much time we had to invest in setting up and attending or exhibiting at these shows. Trade shows were an excellent marketing tool for us when we went to the right ones; there were so many that it truly was difficult to know which would be a good use of our time and money. On average, we exhibited at three a year and attended several others.

If I can make one recommendation regarding trade shows, it would be to request a list of attendees, government agencies and competitors, from the trade show organizer to help decide whether attending is worth the time and expense. Many exhibitors receive the attendee list after the fact as part of their participation package, but receiving it in advance will help in deciding whether attending will yield the possible results sought, making contact with prospects that are already on your radar.

Other marketing strategies, such as publicity, advertising, telemarketing, image/brand building, promotions, collaborations, and, more recently, online/social networking and blogging, are all strategies that can and should be considered when developing your marketing strategy.

Publicity. Convincing media to turn their attention to your business can reap rewards for weeks, or perhaps years to come if the coverage is positive. Earning a profile, or even a mention, in a respected business or consumer magazine can catapult your firm from obscurity to the big time in no time at all. Likewise, a short appearance on a national TV or radio talk show can boost awareness of and interest in your products or services overnight.

Publicity is powerful because it carries with it an implied endorsement from the media giving you exposure; they're writing or talking about you, so people infer that to mean that you are successful and your products and services work. Think about it: if you read about a company in *BusinessWeek* or *Entrepreneur* magazine, your perception of the business improves, doesn't it? That's what you want for your business. Because seven out of 10 people turn to magazine and newspaper articles for information when making a purchase decision, that is where small business owners should be.

To pursue publicity for your company, start by identifying the media your prospects and clients pay attention to, whether newspapers, magazines, blogs, TV, or radio, and then develop a plan to catch the attention of one of those media outlets.

Some of the most popular publicity tools are press releases, which are used to make an announcement; press kits, which are several documents packaged neatly in a folder, providing a reporter with lots of background information about your company; and tip sheets, which are a form of press release that offers tips and guidance relevant to your company's products and services.

Once you have information to distribute to the media, you can mail it out, issue it via e-mail to specific reporters, or use a service such as www.PRWeb.com to distribute it to the national media for as little as $80.

When you start to earn media attention, you may want to create a page on your corporate Web site that features press releases you've issued as well as coverage you've earned in the press. Such a page helps members of the media gather background, confirm that you haven't yet been covered in their paper or magazine or on their show, and see that you are qualified to speak on the topic on which they're reporting.

The only cost for publicity is your time writing up your press releases or tip sheets and distributing them (unless you use a distribution service). So much is done electronically today that you may not even have a cost for printing the information on your office printer. For your efforts, your goal is to receive a call or an e-mail from a reporter who is interested in interviewing you.

In addition to proactively issuing information about your business, you may also want to explore a reactive tactic, namely, finding out what stories reporters are already working on. Sometimes inserting yourself in a planned article or report is much easier than trying to convince an editor to create an article about you. To learn what articles are already being written, you'll want to sign up for www.HelpaReporter.com, which is totally free.

This publicity service links reporters and writers in need of people with specific expertise with experts like you, all at no cost. Sign up to receive thrice-daily e-mails containing lists of stories on which members of the media are currently working. If you find a topic that is right up your alley, respond quickly with a brief summary of your qualifications and initial thoughts on the subject and invite further discussion. The value of any coverage you receive will be worth far more than what you paid (nothing).

For credibility building and cost, publicity is tops. But there are plenty of other lower- and higher-cost marketing tactics worth mentioning.

Telemarketing. As I mentioned, telephoning prospects we had identified and clients we wanted to acquire was our main marketing tool. The primary reason we relied so heavily on marketing by telephone was that it was a low-cost way to make contact with our target market; we didn't have the money to contact people in more costly ways. The benefit was that it opened many doors.

Perhaps what made our approach more effective than most telemarketing operations was our reliance on "warm calling" versus "cold calling." Warm calling involves phoning people with whom we already had a connection, by having worked together, having been introduced through a mutual acquaintance, or knowing them casually or through other nonwork activities. The odds of getting through to someone who knows you, even vaguely, as a warm call are much higher than reaching someone through a cold call, dialing someone who doesn't know you at all. Either way, the payoff, in the form of a face-to-face meeting, can be big. The key is the process.

Each time you pick up the phone, make sure you have an objective in mind. What is your desired outcome if the person at the other end answers? Do you want to introduce yourself? Offer to mail or e-mail some materials? Gather information about an opportunity about which you're aware? Set up a meeting? Or something else?

To ensure that you stay on point and moving toward your objective, consider typing up a script to follow. This is an especially good idea if you intend to have other people making calls on your behalf; a script helps improve consistency of message and delivery. If you're nervous or uncomfortable about making phone calls, having a script in front of you can reduce your discomfort and help ensure that you hit all the major points you wanted to make.

Another tactic is to combine printed materials with a phone call, as a way to warm up a cold call. The idea is that if you mail something in advance, you're increasing awareness of your company that may generate interest in speaking with you. Then at least it's not a totally cold call; you've introduced yourself via the mail and are now following up. Yes, in some ways we are talking semantics here because the phone call recipient really still does not know you, but anything you can do in advance of a call to create a more favorable impression is time well spent.

Keep in mind that planning your marketing strategy alongside your budget will yield the business development results sought, starting with how much it will all cost and how much is available to invest.

BRAND BUILDING

While I believe the previous marketing tactics include the highest return on investment (ROI) activities, they are by no means the only marketing activities to consider. If you have the budget or a particularly innovative approach to a certain marketing method, by all means try it. If your business already has the cash flow to afford a higher investment in marketing, the following activities can supplement your existing initiatives.

Advertising. Because linking brand-building advertising to specific sales activity is nearly impossible, advertising is rarely a smart investment for small businesses. However, there are some caveats.

If you can identify a media outlet (a newspaper, newsletter, magazine, blog, TV station, radio, or outdoor billboard) that your target audience pays attention to, the required advertising cost *may* be worth it. Of course, it's hard to know whether it will pay off until you try it, but studying the demographics of any medium is a smart first step.

When you find a potentially high ROI advertising opportunity, don't jump in with both feet. Yes, you will be offered much better pricing if you commit to a year's worth of advertising, but don't do it. Start by testing a small ad, such as a business-card-size ad or a larger ad purchased last minute from remnant space (leftover space the print publication or TV show had to sell or else run a house ad) to see what kind of response you get. Granted, a business-card-size ad won't generate the same results as a larger ad, presumably because it is much smaller, but it should catch someone's attention. If it doesn't, don't throw more money at it to see what it would take to generate results. You may spend thousands or tens of thousands before you get that answer.

Another thing to consider is that it takes several impressions, or several appearances of your ad, before even your hottest prospects take note of it and make a decision to act on the information you've provided. Statistics vary, but most studies indicate that anywhere between six and nine impressions are needed. That is six to nine individual ads, which will quickly add up cost-wise.

Because of the importance of impressions, do not think that you can buy just one or two ads and generate any kind of meaningful response— that is extremely unlikely. If you've decided to spend the money on advertising, buying nine smaller ads at the same cost of three larger ones is the smartest thing to do. Go for frequency.

Many publications and broadcast media will include design work as part of the advertising contract, which means that you may not need to create an ad yourself. That can save you time and money.

Advertising is rarely a bargain, but if you need to spread the word to a heterogeneous market, it may be the most cost-effective way. On the other hand, if your audience is highly targeted, you will probably be able to find a means of direct communication that is less expensive than mass advertising.

Promotions. Like advertising, promotions and special offers can be pricey. However, when targeted, just like advertising, they can also reap rewards in the form of increased sales and new clients.

Promotions include everything from frequent-buyer programs to money-saving coupons; purchase incentives, such as a 5% discount if payment is received in 10 days; or special events, such as "Kids Eat Free Night." They will cost you money but will not necessarily require any cash up front, which makes them attractive.

The key to evaluating whether promotions are useful for your business is building in a tracking mechanism, such as a coupon code or unique identifier, so you know who responded to your offer. Being able to tie the promotions back to sales can help you assess whether the offer was profitable and worth repeating.

While promotions can work, try to avoid training your clients to wait for a sale before buying. If you make a special offer regularly, your clients may learn to wait for your next deal before buying that item they need. This can end up reducing your long-term profitability, so be careful of the frequency of the promotions you run.

Collaborations. Another marketing tool that can be extremely effective or extremely costly, depending how you set up the relationship, is a collaboration. A very common example is partnering with a respected nonprofit organization to donate a percentage of your sales or profits to support the organization. This can be done as part of a unique campaign that you design together or in support of an existing charitable event. As an added bonus, you could request access to their donor list in exchange for a one-time donation.

As a start-up, you are probably saying, "I don't have money to give"—which is why you shouldn't limit yourself to nonprofit organizations. Look at complementary businesses that serve the same client base or businesses in your immediate area that could benefit from an aggressive marketing campaign. Collaborations can involve as many businesses as you like and do not necessarily require that cash changes hands.

In order to determine whether a collaboration of some kind could benefit your company, refer to your list of strengths and critical needs that you made in Chapter 6. Your goal should be to find an organization that serves the same market but with a different product or service. For example, if you're a home stager, you might partner with a real estate agent to promote each other's services. As a caterer, you might collaborate with a wedding planner to share mailing lists to generate more clients for both of you.

The goal of collaborating is that all participants benefit. If you find that you are not benefiting as much as other businesses, simply look for other collaborators. However, the concept itself can be a smart, low-cost way to earn and give qualified referrals.

Online/social networking. Although online and social networking were not a part of the landscape when RGII was getting off the ground, like collaborations, sharing information and leads with fellow professionals via the Internet makes a lot of sense and is more common today than ever before. Some of the most popular online meeting places today include LinkedIn and Facebook, each of which has its own individual pros and cons.

LinkedIn is a social-networking Web site designed to connect you with others: anyone from potential clients and referral sources to suppliers, consultants, and employees. It is a business meeting place that functions to facilitate introductions between all of its members' professional networks of contacts. In addition to requesting introductions to others, you can invite clients and colleagues to become part of your online LinkedIn network, and you can ask for advice or recommendations from the LinkedIn community at large. If you're looking for a foot in the door at a particular organization, someone on LinkedIn may be able to help.

Like LinkedIn, Facebook also connects registered members with people in their own personal network, but the purpose tends to be more social than business. That's not to say that you can't use it for business reasons, such as announcing new products or job announcements, for example. Facebook is currently better known among the college crowd; however, that's changing, as more small businesses are learning how quickly they can get the word out about their products and services through sites such as these.

The cost of such sites is very low, but the time investment required to really get useful information out of them is high, which is why this strategy is near the bottom of the list of marketing tools you'll want to start with.

Blogging. Similarly, another online phenomenon, blogging, has proven useful in attracting followers, but like social networking, it is also very time-consuming. Blogging is like writing a personal journal for all online to see. "Why would this be useful to a small business?" you may be asking. For some businesses, it's not. However, for companies that are striving to be thought leaders, blogging may be the way to quickly carve out a niche in a particular space without a lot of money.

After registering for a free online account at www.Blogger.com or www.WordPress.com, in a matter of minutes you can set up a unique online address where your blog will be seen. Then, you just start typing. If you're an IT company like us, you might state your opinions about the latest Web servers or rant about the inherent problems with various operating systems. If you run a consulting firm, you might offer your latest white paper on time management misconceptions and include a link for visitors to download the report. If you're a sports writer, you can share your uncensored thoughts on last week's game.

Despite the fact that it is free, blogging is so time-consuming that it, too, should not be one of the first marketing tools you adopt.

A Marketing Budget: How Much Is Enough?

The truth is that because marketing is an important driver of a company's growth, how much to invest in marketing initiatives alone is limited only by how much you have.

Most small businesses with little capital to invest should begin with the bare minimum: collateral materials and a Web site. Once you establish a steady revenue stream, you will need to determine what portion of revenue should be allocated to expanding your marketing efforts. We set aside between 2% and 5% of gross revenues for marketing and business development activities once RGII was actually making money. Of course, Greg's organization wanted more, but we had to work with the limited resources available. Research reported in *The Rogue Marketer* in 2007 showed that "when setting marketing as a percentage of revenue benchmarks, **30% of companies spend between 3–5% of revenue on marketing, with 45% spending over 6% (most of those between 6–10%).** If you are launching a new product, or are expecting to launch into a new market or territory, expect to spend approximately 20% of revenue to fund that program."

Every marketing initiative should have a measurable business impact, energize the sales force, increase demand for products/services provided, and, most important, improve client satisfaction. Let nothing be wasted on ineffective marketing strategies.

I indicated early in this chapter that our marketing and business development activity was an integrated, multistep approach to this organization-wide activity. While many people use the terms "marketing" and "sales" or "business development" interchangeably, in our business, marketing included the activities we initiated that supported our business development efforts. Business development was all about identifying and pursuing specific contracts. Marketing was everything we did to get in front of that prospective buyer. The difference is subtle, but, essentially, marketing came first, followed by business development, followed by a successful contract win. Next up is how we tackled the business development beast.

LESSONS LEARNED

The most effective marketing activities are those that put you in front of your target clients without breaking the bank.

☑ Marketing activities should keep the company's name in front of the client.

☑ Guerrilla marketing tactics, a term coined by Jay Conrad Levinson years ago, refer to marketing methods that provide a high return on a relatively small marketing investment. Examples of guerrilla marketing tactics include publicity, e-mail marketing, and targeted direct mail.

(continued on page 132)

LESSONS LEARNED
(continued from page 131)

☑ At the top of the list of guerrilla methods is publicity, which involves using the media to tout your company and its news. Getting the media to sing your praises is the best use of your time and energy because then you can repurpose any coverage to continue to promote your company: adding it to your Web site, sending out a reprint to your prospect list, adding mention of it in your press kits, etc.

☑ You can market your company without a huge marketing budget, but, generally, the lower the cost of a marketing initiative, the higher the time expenditure required. We spent between 2% and 5% of gross sales on our marketing and business development activities.

☑ Brand-building activities are more long-term focused and may not result in immediate sales. They include advertising, blogging, promotions, and collaborations, among many others. Any type of marketing that helps to enhance your reputation but that doesn't push a sale can be considered brand building.

☑ Before investing in marketing initiatives, small businesses should first be sure about which initiatives will help in generating revenue. Marketing gets the name out but doesn't guarantee that you will get business as a result of doing so.

☑ There are a plethora of marketing techniques; choose the one that's best for your company and that fits within your budget.

CHAPTER 8

BUSINESS DEVELOPMENT

"Ask and it shall be given to you; seek and you will find; knock and the door will be opened to you." — Matthew 7:7

The goal of any company should be growth: growth in revenues, growth in profitability, and growth in market position.

For RGII, growth was achieved through an integrated approach to marketing, discussed in the previous chapter, and through business development. Both are distinct in their roles but similar in achieving the overarching business objective: growth. We grew by communicating and delivering value to the client and by managing client relationships and expectations while delivering results—mainly financial for the company.

Without an effective marketing strategy, business development (BD)/sales would not exist. As a result of our marketing efforts, we used a very methodical approach to BD. By using a clearly defined approach to the BD process, we were successful in identifying and winning a respectable percentage of the contract opportunities we pursued. I say "respectable" because I was never really satisfied with the number of opportunities that we won. Our goal was to win, at a minimum, 50% of the opportunities that had received a bid decision. Historically, we came in around 30%–40%. Achieving this goal was driven by management's decision to have in the BD pipeline contract opportunities with a projected composite value of $1 billion at any given time. Each of these opportunities would flow through the BD life cycle at one stage or another. Our success was due in good measure to the amount of research, prepositioning, and planning we did up front.

PLANNING

Although most small-business owners are eager to jump into researching business opportunities and pursuing prospects before qualifying them, don't. Don't skip the planning process. This process will guide your search efforts when identifying opportunities and will help you to determine which opportunities are right for your company to pursue. You may become overwhelmed by the vast amount of sales opportunities unless you first set up a filter to evaluate the myriad opportunities.

Start planning your BD efforts by zeroing in on your target market. Who are you selling to? The federal government, Fortune 500 companies, or consumers? Narrowing your focus little by little will help you formulate your BD strategy.

Then, within each target market you identify, which contacts are most likely to need and are buying your product/service offerings? Can you describe them demographically, geographically, or by company size? If several markets are being pursued, rank them in order of priority, with the primary market assuming the number-one target position.

Also take into account any selling or budgeting cycles that are specific to your target prospect base. When are they usually flush with funds? When are they unlikely to issue any new contracts? The answers to these questions will help you plan which prospects to pursue first and which to leave for the next budget cycle.

Your planning process is really about clarifying for yourself who your best sales prospects are and then prioritizing which to explore and in what order.

IDENTIFYING OPPORTUNITIES/PROSPECTS

From the start, I knew that my target market was the federal government—about that I was very clear. However, the federal government is enormous. Aiming to do business with the federal government as a whole is much like aiming to sell your services to everyone and anyone; it's just not realistic. I needed to be more focused and specific about which agencies we were going to target at the outset.

Although surely hundreds of potential agencies needed our services, we simply didn't have the resources—the workforce, primarily—to go after all of them. We could end up spreading ourselves too thin and fail to make any meaningful contacts if we took that approach. Instead, we dug deeper by making phone call after phone call to find our best prospects. We wanted to be in touch with people who would lead us to contract opportunities where we had a better-than-average chance of competing and winning.

Our own identification process looked something like the following.

- We confirmed that the federal—not the state or the local—government was where our strengths lay. We listed all of the president's cabinet agencies; there are 15.
- Then, we researched which government agencies, at the cabinet level, had a history of contracting for the IT services we provided. An example of such an agency was the Department of Commerce, led by the Secretary of Commerce, with 12 subagencies or bureaus reporting to the secretary's office.
- Next, we identified the Office of Small and Disadvantaged Business Utilization (OSDBU) within each subagency to learn about specific programs and functions within the agency that awarded contracts for IT services, or we obtained forecast information on future opportunities.
- Because the OSDBU is not a procurement office but serves as a liaison between the small-business community and agency procurement offices, the information received from this office was instrumental in pointing us to the appropriate contact person, or purchasing agent, for our services. We always targeted the Chief Information Officer's (CIO) office because of our IT focus. Armed with names and contact information, we then worked to establish a business relationship with that purchasing office.

Although the federal government is foreign to many small-business owners, the process of identifying a potential client within a given organization works similarly in most industries. For example, in retailing, your identification process could look something like the following.

- Decide on an industry or industries you intend to target on the basis of demand for your product or service. For example, you could go after the cellular telephone industry, the toy and game industry, or men's clothing; the options are varied and underscore the importance of focus.

- Research all of the major companies within that niche. This is your preliminary suspect list. You haven't yet confirmed that they buy your offerings, but you believe that they do. (The *Thomas Register* is an excellent directory for the industrial market, for example.)
- Next, you need to confirm that the information you've gathered about the companies is accurate. For example, do they really buy the type of gasket your company makes? Has their budget for Web design doubled, in fact, in the last year? Confirm what you've heard before you expend significant resources chasing a prospect that isn't a good fit.
- Begin approaching each of the companies to identify the buyer responsible for purchasing your products or services.
- Finally, make contact to introduce yourself and open the door to doing business together at some point. This includes preparing a telephone calling strategy to schedule when and why future calls will be made to keep your firm's name top-of-mind.

Once you've made contact with the right buyer or client, start asking questions to decide whether this is a prospect or client you really want. You're not yet evaluating the qualification but are simply doing more in-depth research before making a decision.

A solid buyer, someone you want to do business with, is someone who has a need for your products or services and who also has the funding or budget to pay for them *today*. These would be classified as near-term opportunities, or "low-hanging fruit," and you will want to move them to the top of your list of opportunities. The work is there now.

A prospect, on the other hand, is someone you want to do business with and who has a need for your company's offerings but who does not yet have the funds available to retain you. The funds may have been requested and will be forthcoming shortly, or they may not even have been requested yet, as is the case with longer-term corporate projects; they're on the drawing board but have not yet risen to priority status.

These contacts you'll want to keep warm with the hopes that they will have opportunities in the future, but they don't require your immediate focus. You need a mix of short-term (tactical) and long-term (strategic) opportunities to sustain your company through its growth years.

CONTRACT DATABASES

So where do you begin to research opportunities? In the government world, a number of online databases announce upcoming contracts of potential interest to government vendors. Several I mentioned in Chapter 4, on government programs, but those most relevant to researching specific government opportunities include the following.

- *www.usa.gov.* Because you can't begin uncovering opportunities until you identify the specific agencies you want to pursue, this site is a good starting point. It will help you better understand how to do business with an agency, where and how to register to be a vendor, specific rules and regulations, etc.
- *www.fbo.gov.* This free site is a place where you can monitor and retrieve contract opportunities that are posted by the entire federal contracting community.
- *www.acquisition.gov.* A free central repository of information about the federal acquisition process, including information about regulations, opportunities, contracts, and partners.
- *www.fedsources.com.* A subscription site that issues contract alerts and provides market intelligence and important federal government news to its paid subscribers.
- *www.input.com.* Another subscription site, hosted by the Virginia based company, INPUT provides market intelligence about upcoming and current contract opportunities to its paying clients.

Before you begin writing checks to the paid sites for information, start with the free ones. That's what we did initially. We couldn't afford the sites that charged for their information, so we took what we learned on the free sites and did a lot of legwork. However, the databases did help. Keep in mind that these Internet sites came later in our growth cycle. Because the "Net" was relatively new, we relied on paper reports received from our target clients.

Unfortunately, the corporate world does not have such comprehensive databases. In the business world, uncovering opportunities happens on an individual basis, by organization, as you introduce yourself to key contacts and they begin to consider you for upcoming projects. After you establish a track record with an organization, you may be placed on a preferred vendor list, which may increase the number of bid opportunities you hear about—but it's no guarantee.

The closest equivalent to the government contracting databases are job and project databases managed by professional and trade associations.

Each and every time you decide to pursue a new government agency or major corporation, this process begins again. Over time, you will become more adept at making inquiries, but the information you need won't change nor will the process.

In many ways, it's like a puzzle. You have to put all the puzzle pieces together in order to find, bid on, and win contracts that leverage your company's strengths. The resources that are available will help you determine which pieces go where and which pieces are irrelevant.

QUALIFYING PROSPECTS

We initially made our list of federal agencies we wanted to pursue on the basis of the experiences, background, and expertise Greg and I had—because we were the entire BD team at first. However, when I left RGII in 2006, there were a total of six BD staffers: a pricing analyst, a graphic designer, a proposal manager, capture managers, salespeople, and subject matter experts (SMEs). However, everyone in the organization was expected to support our BD efforts as SMEs. We had contacts in some agencies and were familiar with the type of IT contracts that they typically issued, so those agencies and contacts were at the top of our prospect list.

Our qualification process early on consisted mainly of prioritizing the agencies where we felt we had the best chance of success. The process then was less about disqualifying agencies than it was about limiting the number of agencies on which we initially could focus. With limited resources, we started with agencies and people we knew and who knew our performance records.

Because both Greg and I had experience working with the Department of Defense, and the Navy in particular, we started our BD efforts there. Although RGII was new, we had relationships with contracting officers and program personnel as a starting point. That was certainly better than trying to break into a new agency cold, where we had never worked and had no existing business relationships. For example, although the Department of Education routinely spends on IT, it was not on RGII's list of prospective clients initially because we had no contacts or experience there. Winning a contract there would have been an uphill battle, even if we had the time and money to pursue it.

Our Bid or No-Bid Process

As we identified contract opportunities, we then subjected each one to a series of qualifying questions. We knew that we couldn't pursue every contract, so we developed the following criteria to identify those opportunities that had the greatest probability of yielding the greatest results.

1. How much knowledge of the client do we have? Do we have a relationship?
2. Does the client know RGII?

3. Does RGII have experience relevant to this particular contract? (If not, should we pursue adding a strategic partner as a subcontractor to the team. Otherwise, we were less likely to continue to pursue that opportunity.)

4. What types of relevant services do we have to offer?

5. What are the client's requirements? (These are outlined in the Request for Proposal document.)

6. What are our capabilities?

7. Do we have the proper skill set and knowledge to propose an effective technical solution?

8. Do we have the resources to submit a viable/competitive proposal?

9. When is the opportunity being released?

10. Do we have enough time to respond with a quality proposal?

11. Who is the competition? Is there an incumbent? If so, is the client satisfied with their performance to date? (The more satisfied the agency is with the incumbent, the less likely we were to pursue.)

12. What differentiates us from the competition? What can we offer that will put us in a better competitive position?

13. What is the client's acquisition strategy? That is, are we bidding as a small business, an 8(a), a subcontractor, or a partner with a larger company? What is the potential return on investment?

Each of these qualifying questions was given a rating of 1–10, with 10 being the highest, on the basis of how strong or weak we felt we were on each question. For example, if we had four months to prepare and submit a viable proposal, we might give that question a 9 or 10 to indicate that we had plenty of time to respond appropriately. However, if the agency issuing the contract had never worked with us, we might give ourselves a 1 or 2 on the question regarding the client's knowledge of RGII. Ultimately, the closer the total score was to 130 (a score of 10 on all 13 questions), the better the chance RGII's bid review board would decide to pursue the contract. The closer to a score of 13 (a score of 1 on all 13 questions), the less likely it would be to approve the allocation of resources to pursue that particular contract.

On the basis of these questions, we then made a bid/no-bid decision, meaning that we decided whether to pursue the contract to the best of our abilities or pass and wait for an opportunity where our odds of winning were higher. The percent of opportunities we ultimately pursued was clearly defined, and we focused on preparing top-quality proposals that often required significant effort.

No matter what market you have decided to pursue, it will certainly be worth your while to develop your own criteria for evaluating new business opportunities efficiently. But to be able to make a quick go/no go decision requires that you prepare a set of standard criteria against which all new business opportunities and deals will be measured.

To craft your own set of questions, ask yourself, "What do I need to know to make a decision regarding whether this is an opportunity I want to pursue?"

Availability of staffing and financial resources is one question you'll want to ask yourself: do you have adequate resources to meet your potential client's expectations? If not, can you acquire them in time to present an impressive solution to the prospect?

Should you set revenue minimums and maximums to limit the types of business opportunities you consider? Doing so may save you considerable time during the qualification process.

Also, your knowledge of the client and your competition is another major area to address. What exactly are your odds of winning? Is your company better than the company currently serving the client?

Take my list of questions and modify them, add to them, delete questions that don't apply to your industry or business, and draft your own qualification process.

PURSUING CONTRACTS

Once you decide to bid on a contract or to pursue a particular business opportunity, the next question is how to win it. What do you need to do in order to best position yourself for this sale or project? It's all about prepositioning and the associated research needed.

In order to effectively pursue and win a new business opportunity, find out as much as possible about that client. If you're dealing with a proposal opportunity, your research will focus primarily on filling in background details about the contract. This may include finding out how quickly the organization expects to award the contract, what precipitated the opportunity in the first place, what problems became so significant as to warrant an outside perspective, and who's expected to be on the short list.

Networking to find out how the client feels about the company that currently has the contract is always worth your while, as is learning what, in particular, the client needs the contract to achieve. For example, are there specific milestones or achievements that the client would expect its vendor to achieve? In IT, that might be information security and data protection; in human resources, the unstated goal might be to reduce external training costs; in manufacturing, reducing shrinkage might be a desired outcome. Find out what second-tier or unstated goals you can include in your proposal that would appeal to the client.

Anything you can learn about what's really going on behind the scenes or who the true decision maker is will improve your chances of being awarded a contract.

THE PROPOSAL PROCESS

As you're conducting your information gathering, after having decided to pursue this new business opportunity, it is time to start working on the proposal document itself. The more complex and lengthy proposals can take weeks or months to complete, so do all you can to start right away. Once the request for proposal (RFP) is issued by the government or corporation, the clock starts ticking. You have only a finite period of time in which to prepare your response.

Start by carefully reviewing the RFP to identify what the client wants and what kinds of format limitations may have been set.

You may learn that you have only 25 pages in which to fully explain your proposed solution, for example, or that the client wants the proposal presented in three separate documents. Be clear on what the client is requesting before you start putting pen to paper.

Next, begin pulling in boilerplate materials you've used in previous proposals. These sections might include information about your firm, your clients, or your key executive team. Little may change with respect to those sections, so copy and paste them into the appropriate section of your proposal early on.

You may want to create a compliance matrix followed by an outline for the document as well, preferably according to the requirements established by the client. Submitting a proposal that is in compliance with the client's directions is key to becoming a contender; ignoring the client's stated requirements will cause your proposal to be deemed "unresponsive," and it may be effectively disqualified. Corporate clients are just as picky; they too expect vendors to follow instructions, so make sure that you know what you are being asked to provide.

Typical sections included in a proposal include the following.

- *Executive summary.* Providing an overview of who you are, what your proposed solution is, and what your competitive advantages are.
- *Technical approach.* Giving a detailed description of exactly what you propose and how it will solve the client's problems.
- *Past performance.* Reviewing the similar projects you've completed for other clients, preferably similar to the one you are currently pitching.
- *Cost.* Showing a detailed line-item breakdown of your price quote to do the work.
- *Appendixes.* Any supporting documentation, such as management résumés, industry reports, articles on the topic, product sell sheets, or other relevant information that does not fit in the technical approach.

Of course, if the organization you are working with specifies a totally different outline, follow those directions. Our example is merely one approach you could take in the absence of other instructions.

When submitting proposals to corporate audiences, your outline might look more like the following:

- Who we are
- What we are selling/proposing as a solution
- Whom we have sold it to before
- How much it will cost
- The benefit to the client

Your proposal's length is largely dictated by how large the contract is, with larger, more complex contracts requiring as many as several hundred pages of information and shorter, simple contracts usually needing only 10–15 pages.

However, in some organizations, including government agencies, oral presentations have become the norm; they may not require a detailed written proposal at all. We welcomed these opportunities! Not only do you save time by not having to write a lengthy document but also being face to face with decision makers can add a new dimension to your understanding of the client. As you make your oral presentation, you can immediately gauge whether what you are saying is of interest simply by the client's body language. We could read those cues. We also got a sense of who they were as people and what their particular preferences and pet peeves were, which often proved useful after we had won the bid.

Many agencies used a process of elimination involving "downselecting," meaning that they would reduce the number of proposals under consideration to the top 10 or top three and then choose the winner from that group of finalists. If you make it to that group of finalists, don't be surprised if you are then asked to make another oral presentation or to provide additional documentation of some kind.

Winning Bids

One reason RGII was often successful in winning bids had everything to do with our prepositioning, the work we did before the RFP was even issued, and what was offered in our proposal. This "prepositioning" with the client gave us a distinct advantage over other firms.

Essentially, what we did was make contact with target clients long before specific RFPs were in the works. Once we received information that a contract would be forthcoming, we began in earnest to learn as much as possible about that agency and our contact's priorities. Our typical prepositioning process typically went something like the following:

- Introduce ourselves to our prospective client early on
- Provide follow-up information on our product and service offerings
- Stay in contact on a regular basis, both to check on the status of any upcoming contracts and to stay top-of-mind with the client
- Gather information on each call to help shape our proposal
- Develop a longer-term relationship that will continue beyond a single contract

Most companies that work with the federal government may make initial contact after a contract has been announced, but few ever stay in touch on a regular basis.

Through our regular follow-up process, on a few occasions we learned that particular bids were coming out sooner than anticipated. This information helped us clear our calendars so that we could respond in time. Other firms that were caught unaware either had to scramble to complete their proposal or had to abandon plans to bid altogether, given the quick turnaround. In other cases, we heard about unexpected bid delays and were able to shift our work flow to compensate for a longer lead time. Those preparatory get-to-know-you calls and visits became invaluable.

Notification that we had won a bid usually came in the form of a phone call followed by an official document, indicating that it was time to schedule a kick-off meeting and begin developing our work plan. The work plan should clearly define how your company will successfully execute/perform the contract, who the responsible parties will be, what the format is for required deliverables, what personnel will be assigned, how the billing schedules are set, etc.

EXECUTION

Now that you've been successful in winning a contract or new business opportunity, the work begins anew—this time on completing the project as promised, on time and within budget. It's all about the proper allocation of resources.

Our first action item was scheduling a kick-off meeting with the client, during which the client set expectations for performance and reporting requirements. During this meeting, you are expected to present your staffing plan and introduce your program manager, the client's primary point of contact within the company. Your main goals in this meeting are meeting the key players, demonstrating that your company is prepared, having the necessary checks and balances, identifying responsible parties, and showing that you're ready to get started.

You may also have a discussion regarding a transition plan if an existing vendor is still in place. Clients may communicate which of the existing workers they would like to retain as part of your contract, which would help achieve a seamless and transparent transition of duties without much disruption. The transition plan will detail not only personnel members and their appropriate positions but also key milestones and benchmarks and the types of reports your new client can expect to receive from you and how frequent. This level of detail will make gauging your process easier for the client.

The fact that you have won the contract has immediately increased your odds of winning a similar contract from this or another organization, as long as you do a good job. Government agencies, corporations, educational institutions, and nonprofits all want to work with companies that have a proven track record and that have performed well on similar tasks for other organizations or that are currently performing similar work for a sister organization. Success breeds success, no matter what the industry.

However, earning a positive past performance reference from a client necessitates that you meet or exceed every expectation. That means completing required tasks on time, on budget, in their entirety—meaning nothing left undone.

Of course, the vast majority of clients understand that no project is perfect. There will be bumps along the way: maybe a key employee quits or needed hardware fails to arrive as expected. Minor mishaps will occur—they always do. Expect them. Clients know that problems will come up, but how you handle them will determine whether your reputation suffers.

To communicate how committed RGII was to client satisfaction, we prepared a "Client's Bill of Rights," which guided our client work. Some of the most important rights were that experienced personnel would be working on projects, all billing from us would be accurate, and we would provide solutions, not excuses. Having a printed document committing to a certain level of performance went a long way toward earning a client's trust. From there, having frequent communication with the client was imperative in solidifying our working relationship. After all, current satisfied clients will position your company for future success with other potentially satisfied clients.

LESSONS LEARNED

Marketing and business development, when integrated, should yield the primary objectives sought: growth and profitability.

☑ Business development (BD) and marketing were terms we often used interchangeably because both functions are so closely linked. While marketing activities kept our name in front of our clients,

(continued on page 150)

LESSONS LEARNED

(continued from page 149)

our BD efforts were more aggressively focused on identifying, qualifying, and pursuing government agencies with contracts that we felt
we had a chance to win.

☑ After zeroing in on a particular market, dig further to find the
respective buyers.

☑ Because it is impossible for any company, much less a small
business, to target every company or prospect in its market, your next
step is to qualify and prioritize the prospects you identified. Which
should be at the top of your list, and which are longer-term targets?

☑ We developed a qualification process to determine which
opportunities to pursue. Every company should do the same.

☑ Free and subscription contract databases will alert you when
government contracts are announced in your field. Sign up for the
free ones first and consider paying for the more in-depth information
at the paid sites after you've won a few contracts.

☑ Most government proposals include an executive summary, a
technical approach, a past performance statement, a cost proposal,
and appendixes.

☑ RGII began prepositioning itself to win a contract as soon as we
learned that an opportunity might present itself. That is, we made
contact with the buyer, informed him or her of our capabilities, and
then kept in close contact about the contract and what the agency
was truly looking for in the form of a solution. This up-front effort
frequently gave us an important edge that led to success.

CHAPTER 9

DEALING WITH ROADBLOCKS

"When you pass through the waters, I will be with you; and when you pass through the rivers, they will not sweep over you. When you walk through the fire, you will not be burned; the flames will not set you ablaze." — Isaiah 43:2

Entrepreneurs face a steady stream of challenges, or roadblocks, during every phase of the company's growth. Just when you feel that you've make great strides and have cleared a major hurdle, another one is bound to be around the corner. Even during the research and planning phase of a new venture, roadblocks of one type or another always seem to pop up. What distinguishes an effective entrepreneur from the not so successful is his or her ability to find a work-around, an approach that solves the current problem or, even better, that anticipates and avoids it altogether. The better able you are to think creatively and get past roadblocks, the more quickly your business will grow.

One challenge I grappled with constantly was how to remain an effective leader in the midst of rapid change within the company. As the company grew, I needed to delegate more in order to stay effective, and yet I couldn't delegate too much; a leader still has to lead. I had to demonstrate the type of behavior I wanted my management team and employees to exhibit, which was difficult during times of rapid growth and change.

Common Business Roadblocks

RGII certainly had its share of roadblocks. Many have been discussed in previous chapters but are worthy of mentioning again here. Some were simply situations I hadn't previously encountered and had to research how to deal with, while others could not have been anticipated. Some common roadblocks that I experienced and that are common to other small businesses include the following.

Access to capital. Finding adequate funding, or access to capital, has been a small-business roadblock to growth for decades and is unlikely to resolve itself anytime soon. Unfortunately, it is also one of the primary challenges to small-business growth. For that reason, it is especially important that small-business owners invest time in long-term planning, devising options for securing needed capital well in advance.

Knowing that landing operating capital would be difficult, we began striving at RGII immediately to improve our odds of success in preparation for the day when we would need additional working capital. Our strategy was to develop a working relationship with our branch manager or senior loan officer and keep him or her informed of our progress and successes, such as when we won important government contracts or moved into new office space. Fostering such relationships was certainly worth the time and effort and worked much better than having contact only with the bank tellers when making a deposit. Funding sources for needed capital were discussed in Chapter 3, so I won't go into detail here. The point to be reiterated here is knowing the importance of maintaining your financial relationships. It eases the process when additional resources are required.

After a couple of years of hearing about your steady growth, your contact should be in a position to support your loan application. Ours was, and that relationship led to a $50,000 line of credit (we were actually offered more and accepted only what we needed at the time).

Insufficient collateral. Loan applications are evaluated on the five C's: collateral, capital, character, capacity, and current economic conditions. Collateral is a big factor because it helps reduce the risk of the loan in the bank's eyes. The more assets you have available and are willing to commit as collateral for backing your loan application, the lower the risk to the bank.

Conversely, a lack of collateral signals risk to a banker. Without collateral, the other four C's become especially important to qualifying for a business loan. Because few entrepreneurs have perfect credit and sufficient collateral, many end up applying for a personal loan or pledging personal assets in order to qualify for business funding. Insufficient collateral is a major roadblock, but securing financing isn't impossible—just more of a challenge. If you can't find a way to qualify for a cash infusion, such as through a traditional bank loan or a line of credit, look for ways to minimize your need for outside capital as a way to work around that roadblock.

We didn't receive the funding we wanted early on because of insufficient collateral, so we used personal credit cards, reevaluated our business plans, and worked to continue solidifying our business base in order to jump-start our growth. We understood that once the company had a history of solid growth, we would generate the collateral needed to qualify for traditional financing. Until such time, we scaled back our growth plans and used nontraditional financing methods to temporarily offset the insufficient collateral challenge.

Lack of clients. Many would-be small-business owners have ample experience and expertise in their industry—experience that has served them well in their career. However, having expertise does not guarantee a successful independent business. Very few clients may actually need what you know how to do. For example, knowing how to run a major piece of obsolete equipment may have been essential to your former employer, but unless that obsolete equipment is in place at other area organizations, you may not have a large enough client pool from which to draw.

Your challenge is finding clients who have problems your solution can solve or services/capabilities they need that you have to offer. In some cases, the solution may be to package your expertise in a new way or to target your services to a new and growing industry. But until you can identify a group of potential clients both with a need for and who are able to pay for your products and services, your company has hit a roadblock on your path to business growth, sustainability, and success. No clients, no business.

Of course, landing those first clients is key, and as a start-up, we worked to convince potential clients (sales at its best) that we had extensive capabilities and the capacity to meet their computer service needs. We had to appear legitimate or we didn't stand a chance. Was that a stretch? Yes, but we knew that we could find the people who could deliver what we had promised, on time and within budget. We had to take the risk, or we risked not being able to win work from other clients.

Once you are successful at securing that all-important first client, small businesses in particular have to make sure their clients are not just satisfied but referenceable, too, that is, that they are so pleased with the work you have done that they are willing to serve as a reference for other potential clients. Unless that client is willing to provide a glowing reference to a new client if asked about your company's performance, that client may be your last. At RGII, my commitment to satisfying our clients included conducting a periodic client satisfaction survey and making personal visits to more than 80 sites each quarter. The survey was instrumental in making sure that the client's voice was heard. The feedback in the areas of performance, quality and value of our services, cost competitiveness, experience of staff, and management involvement and accessibility was a key benchmark for us when assessing client satisfaction. The site visits allowed me to have face time with all our clients to reassure them of our commitment, regardless of the size of the contract we may have with them, get firsthand feedback regarding our performance, and to make necessary adjustments to improve their level of satisfaction if warranted.

Each satisfied client has the power to open doors to other clients, while dissatisfied clients can quickly put you out of business. Having a backlog of satisfied clients, preferably those that are generating profits for the company, turns a roadblock into a stepping-stone toward success.

Lack of performance history. The inability to win new clients seems like a catch-22. Potential clients want to see experience or a performance history, and yet you can't build a performance history without clients. It can be discouraging for a new business owner, but the challenge is not insurmountable—as the owner, you must show diligence, persistence, and creativity.

For example, some small-business owners drop their prices to land budget-conscious clients, rationalizing that there is value in doing the work and gaining the performance history rather than making a lot of money the first time around. Instead, move past the roadblock; sacrifice revenue for a client reference and make up for the loss in revenue with the new clients you will gain as a result.

When appropriate, other small-business owners sometimes offer to do pro bono, or volunteer work for a nonprofit organization as a way to demonstrate their qualifications and develop a track record that can be leveraged to get paying clients.

We didn't go that route but instead tapped our network of contacts in the federal government and worked those personal relationships to get that all-important first client. We had already built a level of trust with them, which made winning small contracts a source of a past performance history as we eyed larger opportunities. However, performance needs to be satisfactory—or better; unsatisfactory performance has a long-term negative effect on growth and becomes a roadblock that paralyzes the company's ability to move forward.

Gaining access to decision makers. In order to make a sale or land a new account, you need to influence the person who will actually be making that choice: the decision maker. Unfortunately, identifying who wields that power can be difficult. You may think that it's the chief information officer, for example, and then learn that it's the department program manager, or vice versa. Getting face time with the decision maker is even tougher when you're unknown to the organization and you don't have an inside contact to make the necessary introductions.

To navigate around this particular roadblock, research the target organization to find a contact within the small-business or purchasing office. A meeting with this person will help you find out who the players, the decision makers, are. Although you may assume that they are senior-level executives, in larger companies, purchasing power rests with lower-level staff members. In the federal government, the program managers are the ones who typically select the best vendor for their needs.

We often requested an organization chart or found it online. From there, we were able to drill down to the department with which we were interested in doing business. After you have confirmed who your target decision maker is, start reaching out to him or her to begin a dialogue. Start with a phone call, then an e-mail exchange, and eventually a face-to-face meeting. Because there is so much competition for your prospect's time, gaining access won't be easy; that is why it is a common roadblock. But not moving past this roadblock will be detrimental to your company's growth and success. If you are willing to take "no" for an answer, you won't get far in business. Being a pest is the key here; people will applaud your persistence in the long run.

Lacking appropriate leadership. The leadership needed to conceive of and establish an effective small business is often very different from the type of leader needed to take the company to the next level of performance. But even before you hit any kind of growth plateau, recognizing the value your senior management team brings to your company is important. Leaders have vision and foresight, which are both critical for helping to move the company forward. Recognizing the roles of leaders and managers will help the owner set realistic expectations for each member of the management team at each stage of the company's growth. I experienced this firsthand when we acquired our first company. We were optimistic about adding new members to the management team and had set appropriate goals and expectations for senior-level professionals, i.e., growth/revenue and profit goals, etc. However, shortly after the acquisition, I realized that what I had gained were program managers with vice president titles.

While substantially growing beyond their existing business base had not been a priority of the previous owner, it was the number-one priority for me as their new owner. This naturally caused some anxiety for the new team members when asked to go above and beyond the level of work to which they were accustomed.

The owner should be able to assess the strengths and weaknesses of each member of the management team. Strengths help achieve goals, while weaknesses, if not corrected, can be detrimental to the company. Making such an assessment can take time, but without strong leaders at every level, the realization and execution of the owner's vision are slowed. Leadership has power, which is why having the wrong skill set can be a major roadblock to a business's success. You can't progress if the people in charge don't understand the vision and/or don't have the knowledge, experience, or connections to propel the company forward. Getting past this roadblock may require a change in key personnel.

This is not easy to do with people who have been with you from the beginning. However, it's a necessity for long-term business success. Remember that the same people to get you to $1.0 million may not be the same people to get you to $25 million. The skill sets are different, so don't try to rationalize it; just understand it and make the necessary adjustments.

Not defining a niche. Some small-business owners think that targeting a massive client base will improve their prospects because the size of their potential market is so huge. In fact, the opposite is frequently true: the more narrowly defined your market, or niche, the better your prospects for success.

Niche markets have many advantages, among them that you can more easily and cost effectively market to a well-defined client group, you can establish a name and reputation faster with a market of 200 than with a market of 20,000, and you will face less competition.

For example, instead of starting a jewelry store offering a broad selection of men's and women's jewelry and accessories, how about specializing solely in engagement rings? Or high-end watches? Or instead of starting a public relations firm, start a public relations firm that specializes in crisis communications or online PR. Not only do you narrow your field of prospects but also you cut out a huge percentage of competitors. Focus on what you are truly best at, and use that as a starting point for defining your own niche market.

For RGII, the federal government was our market, IT services our niche. We didn't do product sales, such as selling hardware and peripherals; we left that up to others. However, we did provide the capability to do the software/hardware installation and integration as part of our collateral duties for networking and integrating the enterprise systems for our clients.

Not understanding industry regulations. Too few small-business owners thoroughly investigate the local, state, federal, and industry regulations that impact them. They may rely on misinformed or less informed friends and colleagues to tell them about which rules apply to them. As a result, they may encounter legal or legislative roadblocks that are hard to move around once they've hit them. Know where these are so you can avoid them.

For example, if your product is under the jurisdiction of the FDA, do your homework before introducing a product—because not only is your product bound by certain rules and regulations but so is your marketing, including your product packaging, displays, and advertising. Don't try to roll out a product without being fully informed about the regulations that impact you. Overcoming that roadblock could be both costly and time-consuming, two words small business owners don't like to hear.

In the federal government space, the Federal Acquisition Regulations (FAR) is the bible. Being familiar with it and knowing which requirements apply to you will save you from facing contract performance and administration roadblocks.

Not understanding your clients' challenges. Unless you approach each client as a long-term source of business, you may encounter unexpected roadblocks along the way. When you commit your company to a business relationship, you should also commit your team to learning as much as possible about that client, including the client's likes, dislikes, needs, challenges, and issues. You want to be viewed as a partner, not just a vendor providing a service or product. A client/partner relationship will better position you to land as much business as possible.

However, if you view clients as a series of unrelated sales transactions, you will eventually face the prospect of losing clients and having to replace them. Depending on your market, replacing lost clients may be easier said than done, so guard your client relationships at all cost. Like most people, clients prefer to deal with vendors (businesses like yours) that they know, like, and trust and that are reliable, deliver quality products/services on time, and are cost competitive. The only way to earn that level of familiarity and trust is if you pay attention to and delight clients; give clients exactly what they need, providing solutions, not excuses. In some cases, they may be able to articulate what they need, and in others, it's up to you to figure that out. The more time and attention you invest in each client, the more dramatic your growth curve will be.

Not developing strong recruiting and retention strategies. Although employees are a company's greatest asset, recruiting and retaining those assets were always a great challenge at RGII. In our industry, IT, jobs are plentiful, but the most skilled workers—the crème de la crème—are almost always currently employed. Wooing them away from a well-paying job is tough, and it's even tougher when you are running a start-up or a relatively new company.

Small businesses rarely have all of the incentives larger companies can offer, although some of the benefits do include great opportunities for growth, the ability to make an immediate impact on the organization, and being regularly recognized for individual and team accomplishments. The inability to recruit effectively can be a constant nagging roadblock to a company's growth, regardless of its size. The only work-around is creating a process to attract and retain the best of the best and developing retention strategies as your company grows. I found that the things that attracted employees the most were competitive salaries, bonuses, paid time off, health benefits (preferably paid by the employer), telecommuting, educational assistance, training, and other incidentals. Without experienced workers to staff the contracts you win from your clients, the clients go elsewhere. Don't let your inability to find skilled workers block your ability to grow your company. Use every available resource to locate the people you need. Some of these were mentioned in Chapter 5.

Not fostering industry relationships. Your clients may be well aware of your capabilities and expertise, but unless you make an effort to be visible within your industry, no one beyond your client base may ever hear of you.

Looking back, we did not do this very well. We were too quiet about our services and qualifications, and we severely limited the number of organizations we joined; we were too selective. In fact, we wanted to be one of those sleeping giants that grew quietly and worked to stay out of the limelight. We could have joined industry organizations and could have participated in industry events, but by staying on the fringe and keeping a low profile, we probably missed out on some opportunities. Ultimately, what we missed out on were relationships that could have been formed that could have directly benefited RGII, such as teaming partnerships to pursue a large client or establishing ourselves in the industry as a leader in a particular service area. Don't make the same mistake we did by trying to stay under the radar. Gaining the right industry exposure has its benefits.

Expecting a handout. Small businesses that approach a potential client, regardless of the industry, expecting to be handed work on a silver platter simply because of the firms' status as a certified woman-owned, minority-owned, or disadvantaged business will encounter a major roadblock. The government, in particular, and its prime contractors, multibillion dollar companies that specialize in serving the government market, have no interest in simply handing out work. Continuing to expect that they will give you work without first demonstrating your capability, past performance, and a competitive price point is a business practice that will yield no results for the company.

Successful organizations want to do business with vendors, including small businesses, with expertise in a particular area—businesses that have a solution or skill to offer. This applies within the government market and the commercial market, too. Instead of asking a client to take pity on you and throw you a project, which rarely works, enhance your legitimacy by bringing something to the table, new opportunities and capabilities, while offering solutions to a particular challenge you know they are having. Proactive problem solvers are respected and hired as strategic partners, eliminating the handout roadblock.

PERSONAL ROADBLOCKS

Sometimes you will face a roadblock that does not originate in the business but that can significantly impact it, such as a health crisis or a family emergency. I faced my own personal roadblock, which emerged in June 1999 after returning from a lengthy client meeting. Within minutes of returning to my office, exhausted, my assistant, Octavia, interrupted me with a phone call from Dr. John Potter's office, the chief of surgery at Georgetown University Hospital.

A few days earlier, I had seen my gynecologist about a suspicious knot on the upper part of my right breast. She wasn't worried about it, and so neither was I, but she decided to be proactive and have it thoroughly evaluated with a mammogram. Because I was under 40 years old, a mammogram was not part of my routine exams, but now it was necessary. The subsequent mammogram came back abnormal, and the grape-sized lump was then removed. The call from his office, which I had been expecting, was to let me know the results of the biopsy. I was not, however, expecting to hear him say that the lump was cancerous. He wanted to meet with me immediately.

I was devastated and confused. How could I have breast cancer? I was 37, in great health, with a very active lifestyle and nutritious diet. I didn't smoke, rarely drank, and was a devoted wife and mother and CEO of a growing company. How could *I* have breast cancer? "I don't have time to be sick; there are too many things on my plate to have to deal with this," I said to myself.

As I grappled with this totally unexpected diagnosis, Octavia comforted me and tracked down Greg, who was in Boston on business. His calming voice on the phone stilled my racing heart as he reassured me that we would fight this together and win. "You must believe that God can heal you completely, so now is not the time to waiver in your faith," he said. I knew that he was right, and while I waited for him to grab the next flight home, I called my sister, Gwen, who is 10 years older. Because all that I had heard was that breast cancer was hereditary, I was confused. "How could this have happened if no one in our family has ever had it?" I asked her. She had no answers but was on her way to be with me.

Now committed to trying to find out why I had to add fighting breast cancer to my to-do list, alongside being a mom, wife, and small-business owner, I decided to call my 71-year-old mother in Alabama. Surely, she could explain this to me. She did.

Having lived by the old "don't ask, don't tell" approach to privacy, mom was not shocked by my news. She was not shocked because her mother, it turned out, had breast cancer, underwent a double mastectomy, and died at the age of 57 from the disease. No one had ever bothered to ask about her mother's cause of death, and she had never thought it important to mention to her four daughters. I was furious with her. Didn't she understand that her mother's cancer predisposed her and her children to the disease? How could she have kept that information from us? Despite my anger, I recognized that it was inconsequential. Being angry would not help me beat breast cancer—which I intended to do.

The next morning at 11:00, Greg and I arrived at Dr. Potter's office for a consultation. I was diagnosed with Stage IIA breast cancer with both invasive and ductal carcinoma in situ, and Dr. Potter recommended immediate surgery but also suggested that I get a second opinion. That second opinion from Johns Hopkins University supported Dr. Potter's findings.

Once the course of treatment had been decided, I had to inform my staff of my diagnosis and make plans for how the company would continue to operate without me. In Greg's and my absence (because he would be caring for me for a short while), we relied on Tom Dunn, our senior vice president of operations, and Chris Parrotta, our CFO, to take the lead. I wasn't ready to give up the reins, but I had no choice. I quickly learned that life would go on with or without me. Fortunately, by that point, the business was stable enough that as long as everyone worked together as a team, I expected it would stay together.

Within three weeks of being diagnosed, I had a right breast mastectomy with reconstructive surgery. Eight weeks later, at the renowned Georgetown University Lombardi Cancer Center, I began chemotherapy, which would last six months. The drugs killed the bad cells as well as the good and made me sicker than I had ever been in my life. The drugs robbed me of my strength—but also the one vain thing I loved most, my crown and glory, the thick, healthy head of hair that I was known for, always having every hair in place. But while going temporarily bald was upsetting to me, I was assured that it would grow back, which also confirmed to me that my body was starting to heal, both physically and emotionally. The diagnosis drained me of not only my physical strength but also my emotional strength. I drew on my faith foundation, reminding myself that Isaiah 53:5 and 1 Peter 2:24 let me know that by his (Christ's) stripes I was healed.

During my recovery, I tried to juggle caring for our then six-year-old twins as well as the company. Fortunately, my staff repeatedly assured me that all was well with RGII. The daily updates helped, too, as I stayed focused on regaining my strength and left the company's health in the hands of others.

Being diagnosed with breast cancer taught me a lot about myself. It taught me to live my life to the fullest, to have faith in God, and not to fall prey to the naysayers who saw breast cancer as a death sentence. I also learned that as much as I loved RGII Technologies, the company would survive whether I was there working 16–18-hour days or not. That was an important lesson to remember even after I returned to work. The year 2009 will mark 10 years for me as a breast cancer survivor. I will celebrate by walking for the fourth time the Komen three-day, 60-mile walk for a cure to this dreadful disease that takes the lives of thousands of women each year.

The last direction-changing roadblock that occurred prior to the sale of RGII occurred in April 2002 with the death of a key employee, Tom Dunn. Tom was RGII's senior vice president of operations and had been instrumental to RGII's success from the moment he arrived in 1995. Tom had gone into the hospital for what should have been a routine biopsy to determine the source of internal bleeding. His visit was all but routine. In fact, Tom would have a major artery severed during the procedure, which caused an unsuspected cancer to metastasize.

Within two weeks, Tom was gone. This news devastated his immediate family and the RGII family, both who loved him dearly. He was a trusted advisor and friend who held the management team accountable, and he was the epitome of leadership at its best.

This heart-wrenching challenge would be one that had no immediate solution. Only time could help us work through moving beyond Tom's death and entrusting this role to someone else.

Challenges and roadblocks come in all shapes and sizes, at the most inopportune times, and each requires action and the attention of the business owner. How to address each challenge is not always as clear-cut as we would like it to be.

PREVENTING AND ADDRESSING FUTURE ROADBLOCKS

While it may be comforting to hear that every company will hit roadblocks at some point, anticipating and preventing them is an even smarter response to the roadblocks you now know are coming. Most small businesses are so short-term focused that they do not take the time to look far enough ahead, to spot the coming challenges before they become major roadblocks. You can't plan for every roadblock, but some are more obvious than others.

The roadblocks you can frequently foresee and develop preliminary action plans for include the following:

- Financial, i.e., cash flow
- Employee or staff related, i.e., recruiting, theft, unethical behavior
- Loss of key team members
- Loss of a client/contract
- Downsizing
- Responsiveness to client crisis, i.e., Y2K

These types of events can benefit from strategic planning in advance. Consider the following:

- The impact of the roadblock on the company
- A game plan to address the roadblock
- What resources you will need
- What time constraints you may be under to resolve it

The quicker you identify and address a roadblock, the better your odds of eliminating it or working around it so it doesn't become a major impediment to your company's growth and success. Doing nothing and hoping it resolves itself rarely work and can make the roadblock higher and wider—almost impenetrable if you ignore it long enough. Such is often the case with tax bills, for example.

However, most roadblocks can't be predicted or anticipated; they simply happen. The current economic crisis our country finds itself in is a prime example. Could you have predicted that financial gurus had set up a house of cards that would result in a near-immediate recession requiring billions and billions of dollars from the U.S. government? If senior economists couldn't predict it—and they didn't—it's unlikely that a small-business owner could be expected to. Yet, you have to figure out how to deal with it nonetheless.

One strategy that works for many business owners is thinking through a worst-case scenario for every aspect of the business. For example, what can you do to prevent the company from going under if your largest client shuts down or moves its business to a competitor? Your answer may be never to rely on one single client for survival. Fill your backlog with a diverse client base and your pipeline with prospective clients to lessen the blow if that were ever to happen.

This process of evaluating potential roadblocks and formulating a potential response or action plan will benefit your company in the long run. Applying the same process in more detail within each department, or with each client, can help you uncover potential problems and work now to reduce or eliminate them in the future. This activity would be similar to the strategic planning process when looking at threats and developing a risk-mitigating plan for each threat. This proactive step moves you ahead in resolving those roadblocks that are identifiable.

It's important to recognize that there are roadblocks at every stage of a company's growth. No matter what the size, businesses face many of the same challenges and issues. The only difference is the scale. A $1,000 tax bill may be just as daunting to a new business as a $100,000 tax bill is for an established corporation. The bigger the company, the larger the roadblocks.

How an entrepreneur copes with adversity can also have a major impact on how quickly and easily a challenge is resolved. Business owners who are proactive, with a positive, can-do attitude, are more likely to move quickly past any roadblock that crops up, while entrepreneurs with a more reactive, pessimistic attitude may expect no solution. Both are right. If you expect to find a solution, you usually will, and if you expect that there is no solution, you'll stop looking and—like magic—none will be found.

Nearly all roadblocks have solutions, though you may need to expend significant resources to uncover them. But unless you've expended every resource while trying to find a work-around, don't consider the roadblock as a dead-end. Most roadblocks are an impediment to growth but not necessarily to survival.

HELPFUL RESOURCES

Should you ever reach a point of not knowing where to turn next, let me share some organizations that may be of help. If they can't help you, they may be able to point you to other resources that can. I gave a lengthy list of useful resources in Chapter 4, but here are some that are particularly relevant to problem solving and troubleshooting.

American Small Business Coalition. www.theasbc.org. This Maryland-based organization's purpose is to foster relationships between large and small companies and the federal government. If you hit a roadblock in establishing strategic partnerships or need guidance in getting a foot in the door, ASBC is an invaluable resource.

Small Business Development Centers. www.asbdc-us.org. To find the local office of the SBDC in your area, check this Web site and then make an appointment to discuss your situation. The services are free and relevant for almost any situation.

Service Corps of Retired Executives. www.score.org. This volunteer organization matches experienced executives with entrepreneurs in need of counseling or practical advice.

In addition to these low-cost options, do some networking to identify local advisors or consultants who may be able to point you in the right direction in your industry or your town. Take the attitude that the perfect consultant is out there for you and odds are good that you'll find him or her.

LESSONS LEARNED

"Character cannot be developed in ease and guilt. Only through experience of trial and suffering can the soul be strengthened, vision cleared, ambition inspired, and success achieved." — Helen Keller

☑ Roadblocks are unexpected challenges that interfere with your plans for business growth. They can appear at the most inopportune times but are generally situations that can be resolved. Some of the most foreseeable involve finance, clients, and employees.

☑ Some roadblocks are totally unexpected. Those are the most difficult to anticipate and plan for, such as the country's sudden economic crash in 2008. Could you have predicted it? It's unlikely. So now your focus needs to shift to how to get past it and keep your business afloat.

(continued on page 170)

LESSONS LEARNED
(continued from page 169)

☑ Companies large and small all face roadblocks at some stage of the game. The only difference is the scale. In many cases, the same solutions apply.

☑ Doing nothing often makes the roadblock larger and more difficult to surmount. Some action—any action—is often better than nothing.

☑ Personal health crises are challenges that will shape how you view your business going forward. They will also demand that you delegate more than you have been. Your own health or family crisis will test you, your family, and your employees as they struggle to live up to your expectations.

☑ By strategizing what roadblocks could occur in the short and long term, you will better prepare your business to deal with them when they do arise. Imagining the worst-case scenario can be a useful exercise and can help you determine how you would respond to various challenges your business could someday face.

☑ Roadblocks do not have to be dead-ends, unless you are unwilling to search for a work-around or solution.

CHAPTER 10

STRIKING
A BALANCE

"From everyone who has been given much, much will be demanded; and from the one who has been entrusted with much, much more will be asked." — Luke 12:48

B alance. We all hear that we need to live more balanced lives and that an unbalanced life is unhealthy, but what exactly does that mean? What does a balanced life look like? In fact, balance means different things to different people. It looks and feels different to each of us, depending on our personal roles and responsibilities.

While you may not recognize when you are leading a balanced life, spotting an unbalanced one is fairly easy. When you are not in balance, your life is chaotic and frantic. You can never get everything done, although you think you should be able to. You are stressed and feel as if you never have enough time for the important things in life, whatever they are to you. Yes, recognizing a state of imbalance is much easier than spotting balance.

Entrepreneurs have an especially hard time with the concept of a balanced life, which to me means spending time and energy on the many facets of my life: spirituality, family, health, business, finances, and outside interests such as my philanthropic and volunteer work. As a small-business owner, it is easy to become consumed with the work and the many things to be done to make the company a success. Many, many entrepreneurs find themselves devoting nearly 100% of their time and attention to their businesses at some point in their lives, to the detriment of their families, personal relationships, health, faith, and personal income. Most of the time, their lives are out of balance.

You may be pulled in many different directions, being stretched thin mentally, physically, spiritually, economically, and emotionally as a result. That is not balance. It takes discipline and commitment to prevent your company from becoming your sole reason for being. For many of us, starting a business is a means of providing for the other people and causes we hold dear. But while you're starting and nurturing your business, you can't completely ignore everything else in your life and expect it to be there once you've achieved your definition of success. Life doesn't work that way.

THE ART OF JUGGLING

Achieving balance requires that you manage your many roles and responsibilities to yield personal satisfaction without feeling overwhelmed or stressed. "Juggling" is the term you've probably heard most frequently to refer to the practice of sequentially or simultaneously turning your attention to the many aspects of your life. Of course, the more balls you have in the air—the more responsibilities you're managing—the tougher it is to be balanced. Staying on top of two or three areas of responsibility is easier than managing 10 or 20. The juggling gets harder as you add even one more new activity or obligation.

As your roles increase, you may feel overwhelmed. One strategy for juggling the many activities and relationships in our lives has been multitasking, attending to multiple responsibilities at once. What we're learning, however, is that it's hard to do many things well simultaneously. For example, if you try to respond to e-mail while you're having a telephone conversation with your spouse or partner, neither will likely receive the full attention and thought from you that it deserves. You may find that it makes more sense to finish the e-mail, hit "Send," and then call your spouse, so that you are fully invested and attentive to each person and each task, rather than spreading yourself too thin.

That is the sure sign of an unbalanced life: feeling stretched too thin. If every activity becomes a burden rather than a pleasure, your life has become unbalanced. You are trying to accomplish too much in the time you have allotted.

Being able to make time for everything that is important to you is balance. You may not necessarily spend an *equal* amount of time on each aspect of your life, but you know what feels right to you. You may spend an hour at dinner with your family, for example, but only 30 minutes at the gym or running outside. Likewise, you may spend 10 hours working on your business and only an hour at church each Sunday, but if that feels right to you, then you are living a balanced life.

If the amount of time you are spending in each area of your life seems off-kilter, you may be trying to do too much in too short a time frame. Those same responsibilities might be manageable given more time, however. If so, one solution is to ask for more time if you can. In general, the more people who are relying on your work or your contribution, the less your chances are of getting an extension; it may also depend on to whom you made the commitment. But it never hurts to ask for more time.

Another strategy is to increase your personal capacity by asking for help from others to complete your tasks, such as by leaning on friends to pitch in or hiring someone temporarily. Maybe some activities don't require your attention at all any more, such as supervising your teenager's homework; he or she may be old enough to tackle it on his or her own.

Take a look at which balls you have in the air as a first step to figuring out which ones you can drop. For example, if you have an activity on your list of action items that has been there for more than a few weeks (and you've just been carrying it forward each day), the need for this work has likely diminished. Maybe you can cross it off or scale back what needs to be done. It's amazing how much additional time you can find for yourself simply by eliminating work that no longer needs to be done.

But before you start crossing off too much, take a step back and assess how your life is going. Is it on the right track?

PERFORMING A SELF-ASSESSMENT

To have a life in balance, you must first decide what you want in your life. What is important and what is not? Do you need a mansion, or would a smaller home do just as well? Is travel important to you? Do you want children? How many? How about the latest-model car—is that important to you? Would you like to find more time to volunteer at the local animal shelter? There are no wrong answers here, just the start of a plan to achieve balance in your life.

Take a step back and look at the big picture, what I call the 1,000-foot view, of each aspect of your life. What is the situation with respect to your faith, your health, your personal financial status, your business, your family or romantic partner, and your outside interests? Where do you stand? How satisfied are you in each area?

Next, determine what the challenge is for you in each area. What is preventing you from having the balanced life you desire? Is it a question of resources, time, or commitment? What is stopping you? What do you need to do to achieve that vision of a balanced life that you have in your mind?

Then, break out the steps needed to achieve your life vision. What would each aspect of your life look like, and what do you need to do to get there? For example, if spending more time with your spouse is important, what would that look like? Do you see yourself taking more weekend getaways? Having more dinners alone? How could you make that a reality? What steps would it take?

If your goal is to quit your current job and start a new business, what steps do you need to take in order to do that? Are there preliminary steps you should consider, such as setting aside a nest egg to tide you over during the first year of entrepreneurship? Will you involve partners? What is your time frame for starting the company? What else do you need? You may find that you actually need less than you thought to get going.

After determining your action items, I recommend making a list of "must-dos." These are standards you set for yourself, which can be as flexible as you need them to be while still allowing you to be happy with your performance in each area. These must-dos help guide you toward balance. Some of my must-dos include attending church on Sunday, tucking the girls in at night, and having a date night with my husband each week. In order to have the balanced life I've just described, these are some of the things I need to do regularly. Without them, I feel more stress.

Some of your must-dos might include leaving work no later than 6:30 p.m. during the week, making dinner every Saturday night, or having a girls' night out at least once a month with your sister girls. Your must-dos should reflect the changes you are trying to make in your current life to more closely resemble your definition of balance.

SETTING PRIORITIES

There is literally not enough time in the day to get everything done. That is a given. Yet we still try to cram as much work and life as possible into the 24 hours we have. We try to do more, to make time for more, but that doesn't improve the balance in our lives; it may even do more damage, by increasing our stress level and feelings of failure. Oftentimes the knowledge that you will never get everything on your to-do list done can be stressful, too. Things left undone cause stress and imbalance.

Now knowing that you won't get everything done—can't get everything done—how will you choose to spend your time? What will you focus on in the next 24 hours? In the 24 hours after that? Prioritization becomes an important step toward a sense of satisfaction and the feeling of well-being that accompanies a balanced life.

Setting personal priorities is one way that immensely helps me manage my workload and family obligations. With my priorities set, I can whittle away my to-do list and feel satisfied with my progress, by tackling the largest priorities first.

For me, my highest priority is always my faith. By putting my spirituality at the top of my list of priorities each and every day, I'm able to maintain a balance of all the other aspects of my daily life. I may not make it to church 50 miles away each week, but I do have time to pick up my Bible every evening and read it before I go to sleep. That sets the tone for the next day and helps me stay on an even keel. Taking time to pray fortifies me and enables me to do my best at the rest of my priorities.

Some days, my priorities may be work related, such as if I have a major presentation to give or a client meeting. They may be family activities, such as watching Brya play varsity basketball or helping Brynn select her next pageant gown. Maybe one of my key activities is taking that run outside that I've missed the last couple of days, to maintain my health.

My health is another top priority for me because it enables me to do everything else. When I'm not healthy, I can't function to the best of my ability. Maintaining my health, by exercising, eating right, and controlling my stress, helps me live a balanced life. My health is also a gauge for how balanced my life is; when my life is out of balance, my health suffers.

Greg's and my personal finances were closely tied with RGII, but I still spent time each month creating a household budget and managing our money to make sure we stayed on top of our bills, lived within our means, and were setting money aside for our daughters' college educations. To spend less time on your finances and more on other aspects of your life, make sure that your focus isn't solely on having more money for money's sake. That's a losing battle because you'll never have enough. If you spend time making your household budget with what you do have coming in, you'll spend less time worrying and more time on the other blessings in your life.

Whether you currently feel you have too many outside obligations or too few, your goal should be to carefully pick and choose how to spend your time with people and causes that give you joy and fulfillment, without feeling that they are a burden. If you find that you are wiped out at the end of each week after countless board meetings, working hard on your business, taking art lessons, hanging out with a group of friends on Friday night, and so on, you may have overdone it. You've filled your schedule to the brim. You're overextended, and, as a result, you are more stressed than you need to be, and you're not benefiting the people and organizations as much as you could if you were less harried. Cut back if some of those activities are starting to feel like a chore.

For example, at one point, I was on five or six boards of directors, but after my family pointed out how much they interfered with the other areas of my life—mainly, spending time with them—I scaled back to just two. Those in your inner circle, your family and closest friends, can also alert you when you are investing too much of yourself in one area, risking burnout and stress.

If you currently have a long list of organizations with which you are involved, consider whittling the list down to a core two or three. If you're trying to round out your social life and want to add some new connections, don't go overboard. Start slowly. You can end up unbalanced again by being too gung ho. Instead, identify some areas of personal interest and then prioritize them, choosing a handful to which you can lend your time and energy. See what your schedule can absorb.

When I plan my daily priorities, I start by looking at what needs to be done first time-wise. What is on my to-do list for today, or what should be? If you don't have a to-do list, first create a master list: put everything on it that you know needs to be done. Then move everything that needs to be done today onto a separate sheet of paper with today's date. Next, rank each activity by importance or due date. What absolutely needs to be done today? What needs to be done today so that you can complete a task tomorrow or next week? Then reorder what's on your list, first to last schedule-wise.

Once you have your list prepared for today, review it to see whether you can realistically get everything done. Estimate how long each activity will take and assess whether you have time to complete everything in the next 24 hours. In many cases, we drastically underestimate how long an activity will take and end up committing to get five hours of work done in one hour. That's not going to happen—it's physically impossible. Yet we create stress for ourselves by thinking that maybe we really can get it done and then being disappointed when we don't.

If you determine that you, like many of us, have overcommitted yourself, look for ways to get help in completing your work. What can you delegate? What can you put off completing? What can you eliminate from the list, if anything?

By staying on top of your rolling to-do list, an action item list you update daily, you will find it easier to be more productive. You'll also complete the most important activities first, which will have the biggest impact on your productivity and personal satisfaction. The more you get done, the lower your stress level. The lower your stress level, the more your life is in balance.

BEING ORGANIZED ENCOURAGES BALANCE

Another way to help reduce your stress level and get more done is to become better organized. The quicker and easier it is to get your hands on what you need, whether a document you need to fax to a supplier or your expense receipts for August, the less time you spend being stressed. All that extra time you find is time you can invest in some other area of your life. Having extra time aids balance.

Most people recognize whether they are organized, but in case you're not sure or you want some incentive to improve your level of organization, let me paint a picture of disorganization. When your office is in total disarray, with boxes overflowing with papers, books stacked everywhere, and miscellaneous mementos cluttering the space, your productivity level is at a disadvantage. It's hard to work when you are surrounded by clutter. It's distracting, even if you know where everything is. You're disorganized.

Being organized, on the other hand, does not necessarily have to look neat, but it should look tidy. Everything has a place: files, papers, bills, pens, equipment, finished products, shipping materials, you name it. The clutter in your life has clearly defined storage places, which makes it easier to keep track of your obligations and work in process.

More important, knowing where everything is, knowing what you have committed to complete today or this week, knowing what is on your calendar, and knowing what you need help with will streamline your work process. When you are organized—not just your papers but when you live a more organized life—you are able to do more in less time. In addition, by planning how you will spend your time in advance, you won't experience the stress of crunch time, that last-minute flurry of activity required to get the work you need done.

Creating Boundaries

One way to force balance into your life is to set boundaries around some of your roles. Do not allow them to overlap. For example, make a commitment to yourself that when you are not at work, you are not working. That is easier said than done when you work at home, of course, but even there, you can close your office door and not open it again until your workday resumes.

Greg and I worked very hard to leave work at the office. When we were home, we concentrated on our two daughters. Making time for them meant that, in some cases, we declined opportunities to get together with friends or were selective about family gatherings we attended. We would have loved to accept every invitation, but in order to spend time with our children and also devote adequate time to ensuring that RGII was successful, we simply could not.

By the same token, we did not want to alienate our friends and family either or suggest in any way that we did not want to see them. To ensure that they understood my situation, I made time to talk with each member of my family and my friends individually, explaining that my lack of participation in our relationships or attendance at events was not a sign that I didn't care about them but simply a by-product of trying to manage a growing business and a family. Once I explained it, they understood. I also did my very best to see them when I could, to stay in touch and catch up on their lives.

However, I did lose some friends along the way, some who chose not to keep in touch and some from whom I decided to distance myself. It was hard for some friends to remain positive around me, and I realized that their negativity was not good for me personally or for the business. Negative people and energy interfere with balance, too.

Greg and I also worked hard at making time for each other. After our roles as entrepreneurs and parents, our roles as husband and wife could have been forgotten too. Some days, we did have difficulty separating work and home; we'd continue conversations we started at work over the dinner table. But most of the time we did a good job of taking time for ourselves, alone. That has kept our marriage strong for 24 years.

If Greg hadn't worked with me, I think achieving balance would have been harder. If your partner is not part of your business, it can be difficult for him or her to understand some of your struggles and challenges and to support your priorities and schedule. Fortunately, Greg and several other key people were part of the support system that helped RGII grow while allowing me to maintain a balanced life.

YOUR SUPPORT SYSTEM

Having your own personal support system is a key component of balance. Unless you have an inner circle you know you can rely on to help you keep your commitments, it will be tough to feel the sense of peace and well-being that accompanies balance. With a group of trusted friends, family members, and advisors backing you up, you can breathe. You have a fallback option if your original plan doesn't go as expected. That fallback plan, that support system, provides a significant source of relief, especially to small-business owners who are so used to shouldering the burden themselves.

At RGII, Octavia made balance possible for me. She stepped in to pick up my daughters at school when a client meeting ran long and shuffled my schedule when a crisis of some sort erupted. When I needed uninterrupted time to finish a speech I was giving, she took my calls and shielded me from distraction. She gave me the time I needed by filling in for me in other areas of my life.

Whom do you have that you can turn to for backup? You may feel comfortable turning to individuals, or even organizations, for assistance. For example, you may not have an executive assistant as fantastic as Octavia to help out with child care once in a while, but you may be able to arrange extended day care for your children at their child care center, or you could pay a family friend to pick them up in a crunch. Having a backup plan, whatever it is, allows you to stop worrying about that aspect of your life—it's taken care of, no matter what.

Similarly, try to arrange backup plans in other areas. If you're worried about a cash shortfall, consider applying for a line of credit to even out the inevitable ups and downs of an economy in transition. Then you can stop stressing about money for a while. If you're not sure that you can make it to the gym three times a week, investigate installing some gym equipment at home, thereby eliminating excuses for why you can't squeeze in some aerobic exercise during the day.

AVOIDING BURNOUT

While you may aspire to lead a balanced life because it sounds more enjoyable than what you're currently experiencing, there is another, more important reason to strive toward balance: it will help you avoid on-the-job burnout.

Entrepreneurs have a higher-than-average chance of experiencing burnout because of our willingness to work extremely hard for extended periods of time in pursuit of success. Our optimistic attitude can become our downfall, by pushing us to continue to work well beyond when others would have taken a break. Yet a break from work is exactly what we need to avoid crippling burnout.

Developing outside interests and setting limits on time spent at work are two excellent ways to prevent burnout. Clear signs of burnout are diminished interest in work, malaise, boredom, and depression, which can all set in when the realization hits that working longer may not make a difference. Unfortunately, once you've overdone it, it can take considerable time to rejuvenate yourself and your interest in your business. During that time, unless you have an inner circle to fill in, the business will likely suffer.

A better approach is to take preventive steps to avoid burnout. Despite your enthusiasm and enjoyment of work, pace yourself. Don't put all your energy into work alone; leave some for hobbies, family, friends, education, travel, or home renovation. Your business and your personal life will thrive.

LESSONS LEARNED

A state of balance helps create the harmony and stability that the budding entrepreneur needs to avoid the physical, emotional, and psychological strain that can result from business ownership.

(continued on page 184)

LESSONS LEARNED
(continued from page 183)

☑ Because we each have different roles, responsibilities, and priorities, a balanced life looks and feels different to each one of us. Balance has no one definition, but the common components of a balanced life include family, spirituality, health, business, finances, and outside interests.

☑ Juggling multiple roles and responsibilities is more difficult the more you add to the mix. Leading a balanced life is easier to achieve when you scale back on some of your responsibilities, if you can.

☑ To determine how to create a balanced life for yourself, start with a 1,000-foot view of your life now. Where do you stand? How would your life look if it were more balanced? Then break down the steps to building that balanced life into manageable pieces. I made a list of "must-dos" that kept me focused on my most important roles and responsibilities.

☑ Then, armed with your steps and must-dos, prioritize your action items from most to least important. Start at the top, but know that you will never get everything done—it's simply not humanly possible. Accept it and do your best.

☑ Becoming better organized will also help boost your productivity, reduce your stress level, and enable you to lead a more balanced life. Disorganization causes stress and creates more work, not less.

☑ Leading a balanced life will also reduce your chances of suffering burnout. When work becomes boring and unfulfilling, you may be approaching burnout, a state of being where you have little or no interest in business. The only way to recover is to rest and relax, rejuvenating your interest in your company. A better solution is to avoid it altogether by building in time away from work from the outset.

CHAPTER 11

REALIZING YOUR DREAM

*"I press toward the mark for the prize of the high calling of God
in Christ Jesus." — Philippians 3:14*

When I started RGII Technologies, my goal was to hit $100 million in sales within 10 years. After that, I decided that I would consider selling the company. That was my exit strategy: where I was headed and the point at which I would consider doing something else.

Of course, the beauty of setting a goal is that you can change it along the way. When Computer Horizons Corp. (CHC) came knocking on our door, proposing the purchase of RGII, we were several years away from hitting our target revenue and from being ready to consider selling. But the offer was attractive, and, at the time, the small-business landscape within the federal community was changing. In order to compete, we drastically needed depth, breadth, size, and expanded capability. Computer Horizons offered all of that, so I decided to sell then. It was time—or so I thought.

You may also reach a point in your business when you feel that the time has come to move on. Even if your original dream or goal has not yet been reached, you may know in your heart that you've taken the company as far as it can go. Maybe you recognize that you've taken the company as far as *you* can take it and it's time for new leadership to come in. In a few cases, the opportunity may have passed, and you have to accept that this particular dream will not be realized. That is the value of having dreams and setting goals: you can mark your progress and know when change is needed.

Stephen Covey advises that we should "begin with the end in mind." That's good advice. Instead of starting a company with plans to help it grow and succeed, Covey suggests being more specific with your goal setting, by thinking ahead to how large you want the company to grow and at what point you will step aside. It's a lot like determining your destination before you start driving cross-country: where are you headed, and how will you know when you have arrived?

Few small-business owners think about an exit strategy during the start-up phase. They're more concerned with the here and now and how to pay their rent this month or make payroll or maybe how to take their business to the next level—not how to sell it and get out. That is probably the least of their worries, many think. It's not a priority.

For many companies, the entrepreneurial cycle may look something like the following:

Year 1   In start-up mode, the company's aim is merely survival.

Years 2–5   It's all about growth and profitability.

Years 6–9   Moving the company to the next level is the goal.

Year 10+   Attention turns to the owner's exit strategy.

Some business owners start to think about the company's exit strategy three to five years into running it. At that point, policies and procedures are often in place as well as a routine that makes it possible to begin planning ahead. That is a smart time to consider what the endgame should be. The entrepreneur should take a step back and contemplate what his or her goals are and how money can eventually be pulled out of the business.

An exit strategy can also evolve as the company matures. If the plan initially was to take the company public in 10 years, but at year eight the financial markets apparently won't support an IPO, perhaps the new exit strategy becomes selling the company to the employees through an employee stock ownership plan (ESOP). Maybe the strategy is to sell to an interested buyer or merge with a competitor. The options are limitless, but selecting the right strategy for your business requires some homework on your part.

Exit Strategies

Although my exit strategy was to sell to an interested buyer, there are several ways to step away from the company you birthed and built.

Acquisition

One of the most common exit strategies is to sell to an interested buyer, as we did with RGII. To get the time, talent, and treasure you have invested out of your business, you determine a fair value for the business and sell it to a new owner.

The most likely buyers are companies for which yours would be a strategic fit, where your company would provide an entrée into a new market, supplement an existing product line being sold to a common clientele, offer greater depth and breadth of capabilities, or help take the other company to the next level sales-wise through the immediate addition of employees, locations, and products. In our case, Computer Horizons needed a platform company from which to launch its federal division. RGII was its medium of entering into the federal government market. Our existing client relationships, contracts, and talented employees provided a huge foot in the door at key federal agencies. For that reason, we were a prime acquisition target.

Other factors that can make your company more or less attractive as an acquisition candidate include the following.

- *Size.* Generally, companies want to acquire businesses that are smaller or comparable in size. Keep in mind that the larger the company acquiring your business, the more financial resources it may have available.
- *Diverse client base.* Providing access to a new customer base can be very valuable to a buyer.
- *Unique distribution channels.* Being able to introduce a company to an entirely new distribution channel for its products and services is another attractive selling point.
- *Varied products/services.* The more products and services that do not overlap with the buyer's, the more valuable your company may be to a buyer, by eliminating the need to do expensive R&D and product development.
- *Strong client relationships.* Perhaps most important of all, your client relationships can significantly impact the value of your company to a potential buyer. The more satisfied and loyal your clients, the more a buyer may be willing to pay in order to tap into that loyalty.

Even when you see a strategic fit, agreeing on a purchase price can be tricky. Your goal as the seller is to receive your asking price, the company's market value or better, although in many cases the owner's perceived value is quite different from what the market indicates the company is worth; many owners assume that the value is much higher. Unfortunately, insisting that the company is worth much more than market value will limit interest from buyers, who want to pay as little as possible, preferably below market value. Yes, some buyers will pay more than market value when the acquisition of your company will give them a significant competitive advantage, but don't assume that that will always be the case.

Merger of Equals

Besides selling, merging your company with another to become a single entity is an option. However, synergy and a strategic fit between the two companies are even more important when two businesses are being combined than when one is buying another.

Mergers are a smart way to increase a company's market presence and potentially enable it to capture a larger market share, bolstered by the resources and capabilities of its merger partner. They can also be very lucrative to the company being targeted for a merger, though typically less money is paid up front to the seller; the potential for earnings comes later, as the combined entity thrives.

Initial Public Offering

A popular exit strategy until a few years ago, when the cost of an initial public offering (IPO) soared, "going public" is one way to generate funds and facilitate your exit from the business. An IPO provides potential investors with the opportunity to buy into the company at a set stock price, taking ownership of the company. That's how money is generated for the company and for you, the owner and presumably the largest stockholder. When the value of the stock increases, everyone makes money, including you.

However, it's hard to know how the stock market will react to each IPO. Some are huge successes while others languish until the stock is eventually delisted and taken off the exchange. That's one of the potential downsides of an IPO: an uncertain future. The whole IPO process is also very expensive, and few small businesses have the financial resources to afford this route.

NEXT-GENERATION OWNERSHIP

While a succession plan should be part of any business's operating plan, it is essential if your exit strategy is to pass it down to your children or grandchildren. Identifying and grooming a successor is crucial in such instances because preparation for a leadership role can take years, even if that role isn't CEO (such as COO or CFO, for example). Family members also need to know whether they are in line to receive control and to confirm that they actually want it; some may not.

Although a number of events can trigger the official passing of the baton, the most common are the following:

- Retirement
- Death
- Incapacitation
- Divorce

If your goal is to extract some of your initial investment when the ownership changes, you can work out a buyout plan; in such cases, you may continue to draw a salary for a set number of years or until a certain dollar amount has been paid out or some combination thereof. Being flexible about payment arrangements, while still holding the new owner to certain terms, can also help the new owner make a go of it.

EMPLOYEE STOCK OWNERSHIP PLAN (ESOP)

If you have no children, grandchildren, siblings, nieces, or nephews interested in assuming your business, you may want to consider selling the company to your employees or to your management team. Such a process of selling ownership shares in the company to employees is called an ESOP, or employee stock ownership plan.

Rules and regulations dictate how such a transfer of assets should occur, and you'll want to investigate them with the help of your attorney and accountant. An ESOP can be a smart way to reward loyal employees and keep the company operating while still receiving a payout for your efforts. You may also see tax benefits from transferring ownership versus an upfront payout. Check with your accountant.

WALK AWAY

In some cases, when a buyer doesn't appear and the next generation isn't interested in taking over the company, your best option may be to walk away from it. In a nutshell, that involves paying off any debts; liquidating your assets, such as inventory and equipment; and closing the doors. It's a way to move on, hopefully with some cash from the sale of the assets, to tide you over until you decide what to do next, if anything.

This strategy makes the most sense when a business has come to a natural end. Maybe the generation that used to buy from you no longer does or the industry has shifted to such a degree that demand for your services no longer exists. In such cases, you may opt to communicate your plans to your clients and then work toward a *profitable* end to the business. The profitable part is important—don't just give your assets away. After all, you were in business to make money.

Now you can start over in a new business or opt to become an employee somewhere else—but the business will no longer exist. That's another important difference: when you sell the company, it continues to live on in one form or another, but if you shut it down, it's closed for good.

LIMITED OPTIONS

However, not all companies have these exit strategies available, namely, lifestyle companies. These are businesses that were established with the primary goal of supporting the lifestyle of the owner.

While they are formed like many other businesses and can be in any industry or market, lifestyle ventures have limited growth potential. In some cases, such companies are established around the owner's talents and skills, with little opportunity for involvement from others. A one-person business is often hard to sell, though it may provide very well for the entrepreneur's salary.

However, lifestyle companies also have limited salability due to the owner constantly taking income out to support his or her personal lifestyle. If income is not reinvested to support the company's growth, expansion is difficult. The owner is bleeding the company of its assets rather than using the money it takes in to foster additional growth. Consequently, fewer exit strategies are available to these types of businesses, because few significant assets are ever acquired.

IS THIS THE RIGHT TIME TO SELL?

Despite having planned for a specific exit, many entrepreneurs feel some sense of anxiety and doubt when the opportunity finally presents itself or when the time feels right. Having spent years building your business, are you ready to let it go? Let's look at some of the pros and cons of exiting your business in one way or another.

PROS

- You get to reap the benefits of your time, talent, and treasure. All your years of hard work are coming to fruition or completion.
- You can pursue other interests without continuing to be responsible for the company.
- With the funds or the time you now have available to you, you can start a new company.

- You may now have additional financial resources available to you to start that new business, to retire, to move, or to pursue other interests for which you haven't had time.
- Selling, merging, or pursuing an IPO can give you a huge feeling of accomplishment. You built something of value, employed others, and contributed to the economic base of your town or state. Those are things of which you can be very proud.

Cons

- Of course, by exiting your business, you are giving up control of your "baby," your venture. It won't be yours any longer.
- Not having to go to work each day can lead to questioning your sense of purpose. What are you supposed to do now? Unless you have a postsale plan, it may take some time to sort out the answer.
- Selling or leaving a company can lead to separation anxiety. After spending day in and day out at your business, not having to go in each day can be difficult. You will probably miss your employees and coworkers, too, many of whom may stay on after you go.
- Almost immediately, you may start second-guessing yourself. Did you make the right decision? Was this the best time to sell?

Many of the feelings of elation and sadness will dissipate as you develop a postsale routine. The more planning you do in advance, to determine how you'll spend your time and newfound resources, the fewer negative feelings may remain.

Ultimately, you have to decide for yourself whether the time is right for you to leave and move on to other activities. Considering the economy, your company's past and future potential performance, the stage of life you are in, your future goals, and any other factors important to you, all you can do is make a decision based on what you know now. You don't know what the market will do next week or next year.

You don't know whether your management team will still be in place in a few months or whether all your client relationships will remain strong. There are so many unknowns that all you can do is decide for today whether the opportunity before you feels right.

If you decide that the time may be right, then you start to negotiate the terms of a sale or handoff.

NEGOTIATING THE DEAL

No matter what your ultimate exit strategy may be, there are always details to be negotiated. Whether it's the purchase price, the payment terms, the amount paid up front versus over time, a management contract, targets during the transition period, a noncompete clause, or some other aspect of the deal, be prepared to evaluate all your options and to propose new approaches.

One of the biggest factors—plain and simple—is the money. If you are selling to another company, you might receive a cash payment in full or in part, or you might receive all stock in the buyer's company, or you may agree on some combination of the two. That's what you need to negotiate, on the basis of your financial needs and your knowledge of and confidence in the buyer's ability to take your company and make it even more successful than it has been under your leadership. The more confident you are, the more you may be willing to take in stock, with the obvious potential for appreciation of that stock over time. The buyer, of course, would prefer to give you all stock and no cash, in most cases.

But the sale of your biggest asset is only one component of the deal. Another is your continued employment as part of a management transition team: how long is that transition period? You probably want a short-term employment contract; they may want several years. You negotiate.

In many companies, employees are a valued asset; keeping them on board and the business intact is critical for obtaining the highest purchase price. As you begin negotiations with a buyer, one of your most important jobs as business owner will likely be selling the idea of being bought to your management team. The buyer may even ask all upper management to sign contracts to stay on for a set period of time, to ensure a smooth transition.

How much you'll receive in salary, perks, and bonuses is also up for negotiation. The buyer may want to require that you reach certain performance targets in order to qualify for compensation. Again, you negotiate.

Unless your company is being bought by a company already in your industry, your management team will likely be needed for a transition period. If you are being bought by a competitor, however, that transition period may be short-lived.

Most sellers, if they stay on postacquisition, ask for, and many receive, "golden parachute" clauses as part of the sale, which stipulates that if the company is sold again, you receive all the benefits due to you and can walk away without further obligation.

Having a skilled attorney is key to protecting your interests. He or she knows what is typical for a contract of the size you are negotiating and can propose better terms than you might think of. You'll certainly want to retain a business lawyer experienced in the purchase and sale of companies of your size.

Valuing Your Business

While many factors must be negotiated, the biggest, of course, is the purchase price for your company. The process of determining its fair market value is a valuation, which is typically performed by an accountant or valuation specialist, much like a home appraiser examines a home for sale. Unfortunately, there is no one way to estimate a company's value. Even within a single industry, different approaches to valuing a business can result in a different figure. Your accountant or business broker can tell you which method is likely to bring you the highest price and which is most fair.

The most common approach is to take a multiple of annual profits. Another strategy involves looking at earnings before interest, taxes, depreciation, and amortization (EBITDA) as a measure of the company's operation cash flow and a strong indicator of its profitability.

But the business's net income, annual revenue, cash flow, and the value of its assets can also play a major role in determining a company's value.

How the company fits into the buyer's future plans, however, may be the biggest factor of all. A company desperate to enter your marketplace quickly may be willing to pay a premium for speed. On the other hand, a competitor may not be willing to pay full value for property, plant, and equipment that duplicate what it already has, reducing what you might receive as an offer.

Each situation is different and distinct and will depend on the buyer's and seller's priorities—which may not always be financial.

Dreams Come with a Price

Although I'm very proud of RGII and what our team accomplished, building a highly respected IT services company generating nearly $50 million in sales, there are some things I wish had known about the process of selling a company. For example, I wish I had known more of the legal lingo that the many attorneys were batting around during the negotiations. The massive amount of paperwork was overwhelming, and I'm not convinced that I asked all of the right questions, or I wish that I had at least asked more questions.

I also wish that I had understood the impact of not being in the driver's seat and how I would feel about that. Let me tell you: it's quite a switch. My status changed completely and abruptly after the sale of RGII. I expected that opportunities would come flooding in after word of our big sale got out, but they didn't. I adjusted, but I wish that my expectations had been more realistic.

With the benefit of 20/20 hindsight, I wish that I had taken a closer look at the four-year noncompete agreement I signed. Computer Horizons absolutely insisted on having one—it was a deal breaker—and initially demanded a five-year term. I hesitated to sign one longer than three years, but we settled on four, and the sale proceeded. Looking back, I wish I had recognized how long four years is in the business world; it feels like an eternity. However, what this time away from the hustle and bustle of business ownership has done is allowed me to pursue other interests. Writing this book is a prime example of why things happen for a reason.

I also wish I had waited a little longer to sell the company, to try to hit our original $100-million target. To do that would have challenged us to develop a new set of growth strategies and tactics; I think I would have enjoyed the learning process. But I know that had we waited, we would have faced fierce competition and new legislation that would have hindered our ability to grow as a small business. We were too small to be big and too big to small, so waiting was not necessarily the best option for us at the time.

In the end, however, what I did learn I know will help me in the future, whether I decide to start a new venture or take the helm at an existing company.

LESSONS LEARNED

Entrepreneurship is a journey that requires a specified destination—a well-thought-out exit strategy with a return on investment of time, talent, and treasure.

☑ Start a business "with the end in mind," meaning that from the beginning, you should think about how you may want to end your involvement with the company.

☑ Once you get past start-up mode in your business, it is not too early to consider your exit strategy. Three to five years into running a business is a typical time frame to start charting your exit.

(continued on page 199)

LESSONS LEARNED
(continued from page 198)

☑ The most common exit strategies include sale, merger, IPO, ESOP, handing down to the next generation, or shutting it down.

☑ However, if you've created a lifestyle business, one based on your personal skills and talents designed solely to support your lifestyle and expenses, it will be more difficult to sell or hand down. Your options will be more limited.

☑ Setting a growth or revenue target will help you decide when the time is right to sell the business or extricate yourself in other ways. You can also measure your progress along the way.

☑ If you are presented with the opportunity to sell, as we were, to merge, or some other method to divest yourself of the business, you'll want to be sure that you have an accountant and experienced business attorney in your corner. Many aspects of the deal need to be negotiated, including the price, timing, transition period, noncompete clause, and many other issues that may be important to the buyer.

☑ You will probably never be sure that the time is right or the price is right, and you will likely have regrets later on even if you negotiate the best possible deal ever. These feelings are natural given the amount of time and energy you have invested in making your business what it is today. But look ahead to the opportunities that you now have before you, and try not to look back.

EPILOGUE

"And whatever you do, whether in word or deed, do it all in the name of the Lord Jesus, giving thanks to God the Father through him." — Colossians 3:17

The thermometer registers 87 degrees here in Tampa, Florida, in the middle of December 2008. The temperature here is quite different from the 60 degrees I left in Maryland, which is unseasonably warm there even for this time of year. Since I started writing this book, I have been here four times, and each time I am more inspired. Therefore, I thought it appropriate to finish writing the book I have longed to write for the past 10 years here in Tampa, overlooking the pristine Tampa Bay.

Navigating Your Way to Business Success: An Entrepeneur's Journey has been a labor of love and gives me a great sense of personal accomplishment. Being an entrepreneur was not my initial career path. I do not believe I was born an entrepreneur, but I do believe that I wear the badge of entrepreneurship well, much like a pair of fine, handcrafted leather boots.

To every journey there is a season. My entrepreneurial journey cast me into a season that forced me to stretch myself beyond the realms of what my mind could conceive. The journey placed me in the lives of people who impacted me in more ways than they realized. The adage is true that companies don't succeed—the people do. Without the contribution of each employee, client, bank, consultant, and advisor, as well as family, friends, other acquaintances, and the divine will of God, RGII would have never achieved what it did.

In the minds of some, RGII may appear that it wasn't enough to write a book about. But to those entrepreneurs who doubt the sensibility of it all, I hope that you have been inspired and encouraged by the small glimpse into my journey as an entrepreneur.

Being an entrepreneur was not just my job; it was who I became, and now I am convinced that I will always and forever be an entrepreneur.

It's been nearly six years since I sold RGII Technologies to the now-defunct Computer Horizons and three years since I walked out of its doors for the last time. I still miss it, mainly on the days when I wake up and realize that the next eight or nine hours aren't already scheduled for me. I miss the talented people with whom I had the true privilege to work. They made RGII the success that it was.

Post-RGII, I must admit that my life is still balanced. There have been a few bumps here and there, but for the most part, I am less stressed and much more focused on family and philanthropic pursuits, which RGII made possible.

I am on the boards of directors of several organizations and have established a number of endowments and scholarship programs, including the Richard Gregory Freeland II Scholarship Program, the Kathryn B. Freeland Scholarship at the University of Alabama at Birmingham, and the R. Gregory and Kathryn B. Freeland Scholarship Fund at the University of Maryland, Baltimore County.

To stay connected to the small-business community and provide mentoring and consulting services, I founded Freeland and Associates LLC in 2007. To spread my message to other entrepreneurs—that "yes, they can do it"—I speak frequently at conferences and educational workshops nationwide. Greg, to whom I have been married for 24 years, also started a new business venture, FI Holdings Inc. He too will always be an entrepreneur.

Together, we are preparing to be empty nesters in a couple of years, when both Brya and Brynn head off to college. They are both currently high school sophomores, so college is a major focus at the moment for them and for us. Brya is an honor student with athletic prowess demonstrated on the basketball court. A member of the prestigious Amateur Athletic Union (AAU), she plays basketball 11 months of the year. Her college plans include a dual degree in engineering and business management at UNC. One day she hopes to be an entrepreneur. Brynn too is an honor student, in addition to being a talented pianist and a former Miss Maryland Pre-Teen. She plays competitive volleyball and will travel to Italy in the summer of 2009 to play internationally. Her sights are set on Katie Couric's job, as she hopes to earn a dual degree in broadcast journalism and mass communications from USC.

Any regrets? I have been asked this question numerous times. I do have a few. I sometimes regret the timing of the sale of RGII. Selling it was our exit strategy from the beginning, but when the offer from Computer Horizons landed on my desk a few years earlier than anticipated, we felt like the time was right to move on. Looking back, I think that was premature. Maybe that's the separation anxiety talking, but I think that most entrepreneurs feel that way after they sell the companies they founded and nurtured, that they could have done so much more had they stayed. But that's in the past now.

I encourage my entrepreneurial cohorts to enjoy the journey and all that business ownership has to offer.

"For the vision is yet for an appointed time, but at the end it shall speak, and not lie; though it tarry, wait for it; because it will surely come, it will not tarry." — Habakkuk 2:3

I am truly blessed.

APPENDIX

To help you get started on your own entrepreneurial journey, I've compiled a list of all of the resources I mentioned in the book, as well as other books, organizations, programs, and online resources I recommend.

BOOKS

BUSINESS PLANNING

Building Your Business Plan: A Step-by-Step Approach by Harold J. McLaughlin

Hope Is Not a Strategy by Rick Page

Blue Ocean Strategy by W. Chan Kim and Rene Mauborgne

Hope Is Not a Method by Gordon R. Sullivan and Michael V. Harper

BUSINESS GROWTH

For Entrepreneurs Only: Success Strategies for Anyone Starting or Growing a Business by Wilson Harrell

Succeeding against the Odds by John H. Johnson

Execution by Larry Bossidy and Ron Charan

Keep What's Good, Fix What's Wrong and Unlock Great Performance by Gary Neilson and Bruce A. Pasternack

LEADERSHIP

Secrets of Effective Leadership by Fred A. Manske Jr.

The Effective Executive by Peter Drucker

Principle-Centered Leadership by Stephen R. Covey

Succeeding in Business without Losing Your Faith by Edward R. Dayton

Permission to Win by Ray Pelletier

Jack Welch and the 4 E's of Leadership by Jeffrey A. Krames

EMPLOYEE MANAGEMENT

The ABC's of Building a Business Team That Wins by Blair Singer

Gung Ho: Turn on the People in Any Organization by Ken Blanchard and Sheldon Bowls

Who Moved My Cheese? by Spencer Johnson MD

Hire the Best and Avoid the Rest by Michael Mercer

MARKETING

Marketing Insights from A to Z by Philip Kotler

Speak Like a CEO by Suzanne Bates

SALES

Strategic Sales Leadership: Breakthrough Thinking for Breakthrough Results by the Sales Educators

Think Like Your Customer: A Winning Strategy to Maximize Sales by Understanding How and Why Your Customer Buys by Bill Stinnett

How to Become a Rainmaker: The Rule for Getting and Keeping Customers and Clients by Jeffrey J. Fox

Differentiate or Die: Survival in Our Era of Killer Competition by Jack Trout

Branded Customer Service: The New Competitive Edge by Janell Barlow and Paul Stewart

ORGANIZATIONS

American Small Business Coalition. www.theasbc.org

Business Incubators.
http://www.nbia.org/resource_center/links_to_member_
incubators/index.php

Chamber of Commerce (in your area).
www.uschamber.com/sb/default.htm

Economic Development Corporation (in your area).

Export-Import Bank of the U.S (Ex-Im Bank).
www.exim.gov/smallbiz/index.html

Internal Revenue Service (IRS). www.irs.gov

Minority Business Enterprise Centers (MBECs).
www.mbda.gov

Minority Business Opportunity Centers (MBOCs).
www.mbda.gov

National Minority Supplier Development Council Inc.
www.nmsdcus.org/

Native American Business Enterprise Centers (NABECs).
www.ncaied.org/native-american-business-enterprise.php

Procurement Technical Assistance Centers (PTACs).
www.dla.mil/db/procurem.htm

Small Business Administration (SBA). www.sba.gov

Service Corps of Retired Executives (SCORE).
www.score.org/findscore/index.html

Small Business Development Centers (SBDCs).
www.asbdc-us.org

Small Business and Technology Development Center (SBTDC). http://www.sbtdc.org/services/sell_fedgov.asp

U.S. Library of Congress. http://thomas.loc.gov

Women Business Centers (WBCs).
www.sba.gov/idc/groups/public/documents/
sba_program_office/sba_pr_wbc_ed.pdf

BUSINESS DEVELOPMENT PROGRAMS

8(a) Business Development Program.
sba8a.symplicity.com/applicants/guide

HUB Zones. https://eweb1.sba.gov/hubzone/internet/index.cfm
http://map.sba.gov/hubzone/init.asp

Small Business Innovation Research Grants.
www.sba.gov/SBIR

ONLINE RESOURCES

Blogging.
www.blogger.com
www.wordpress.com

Business Plan Templates. www.freebusinessplans.com

Code of Federal Regulation (CFR).
www.gpoaccess.gov/cfr/index.html

Credit Report. www.annualcreditreport.com

Dun and Bradstreet. www.dnb.com

Federal Acquisition Regulation (FAR). www.arnet.gov/far

Financing.
    www.activecapital.org
    www.nvca.org
    http://www.sba.gov/SBIR

Government Contracting.
    www.acquisition.gov
    www.ccr.gov
    www.fbo.gov
    www.fedsources.com
    www.fose.gov
    www.fpds.gov
    www.input.com
    www.usa.gov

Hiring/Résumés.
    www.careerbuilder.com
    www.dice.com
    www.monster.com

Online Networking.
    www.facebook.com
    www.linkedin.com

Publicity Distribution.
    www.prweb.com
    www.helpareporter.com

Salary Guides.
    www.imercer.com
    www.payscale.com
    www.salary.com

Thomas Register.
    www.thomasnet.com

Web Design
    www.elance.com
    www.rentacoder.com

ABOUT THE AUTHOR

K athryn B. Freeland is founder and former chief executive officer of RGII Technologies Inc., an information technology, systems integration, and engineering solutions company that served nine presidential cabinet agencies of the federal government. Freeland successfully built and sold RGII to Computer Horizons Corp. in 2003. After fulfilling a three-year transition period with Computer Horizons, she retired in 2006.

As the CEO of RGII, Freeland was directly responsible for developing goals, operating plans, and policies for the corporation and implementing board-approved plans. She directed the company with a strategic business plan designed to optimize profits and return on invested capital. During her tenure as CEO, Freeland played a vital role in business development, customer satisfaction, financial stability, and employee relations. During that time, RGII more than tripled in size, with revenue growing 4,800% during an 11-year period.

Prior to founding RGII, Mrs. Freeland spent more than seven years supporting various federal government agencies in the areas of financial, information, and program management support. Freeland is a visionary leader who has made her mark in the business community.

Freeland now serves as the founder and chief executive officer of Freeland and Associates LLC, a consulting services firm that partners with businesses in the areas of executive advisory services, interim executive support, strategic planning/mapping, market analysis/penetration, financial/accounting management, business integration/transition, and business development.

Freeland remains active in several local, regional, and national organizations. Her current and previous board appointments include the following:

- Board of Directors, Black Women in Sisterhood for Action (BISA)
- Board of Visitors, University of Maryland, Baltimore County (UMBC)
- Board of Directors, Baltimore Washington Medical Center (BWMC), formerly North Arundel Hospital
- Board of Directors, University of Maryland Medical Systems (UMMS)
- Board of Trustees, Anne Arundel County Retirement and Pension System
- Board of Directors, Anne Arundel Economic Development Corporation (AAEDC)
- Board of Directors, Girl Scouts of Central Maryland

Among her notable achievements are the following:

- 2007 TWIN Awardee: YWCA of Annapolis and Anne Arundel County
- 2006 Top Technology Entrepreneur by Black Engineers of America
- 2006 Maryland Top 100 Women
- 2003 Selected as one of six successful business owners to be honored during SBA's fiftieth-anniversary celebration
- Leadership Maryland Class of 2003
- Maryland's Top 100 Women for 2003
- Outstanding Alum by her alma mater, the University of Alabama at Birmingham, where she has established the Kathryn B. Freeland Endowment for minority and under-privileged students pursuing degrees in the field of finance at UAB
- Established the Richard Gregory Freeland II Scholarship Program in memory of her deceased son, supporting minority

students in the areas of computer science, information management, engineering, business management/administration, telecommunications, or other technology-related fields

- Established the R. Gregory and Kathryn B. Freeland Scholarship at the University of Maryland, Baltimore County, supporting students majoring in the areas of information technology or computer engineering within the Meyerhoff Scholars Program
- 2002 *Baltimore Business Journal* Forty under 40
- 2001 TechnoRising Star Award for Woman-Owned Business by Maryland's Department of Business and Economic Development
- 2001 Industry Information Technology Award for Top Minority-Owned Firms by PostNewsweek Technology Group
- 2000 Black Woman of Courage: Emerging Business Award by the National Federation of Black Women Business Owners (NFBWO)
- *Black Enterprise* Magazine 1999 Emerging Company of the Year
- *The Network Journal* 1999 Forty and Under 40 Award for excellence in business achievement
- Finalist in the highly coveted Ernst and Young Entrepreneur of the Year Award competition
- Named the Minority Small Business Person of the Year by the Small Business Administration in 1995

Freeland also holds membership in various professional organizations and is a sought-after speaker. Speaking engagements include the following:

- University of Alabama at Birmingham, Honors Convocation Speaker
- Panelist on the topic of Global Trends in Technology, Propelling Women into Leadership, sponsored by the Centers for Women

in Technology at UMBC in conjunction with the Maryland Department of Business and Economic Development

- Keynote speaker at Wake Forest University Babcock Leadership Series
- UMBC Alex Brown Center for Science and Technology Entrepreneurship Speaker Series on the topic "Entrepreneurship: More Than a Notion"
- University of Maryland's Robert H. Smith School of Business Entrepreneurship Club
- DuBois Business Summit on Survival and Success

Freeland holds a master's degree in business administration with a concentration in financial management from the University of Maryland, College Park, and a Bachelor of Science degree in finance from the University of Alabama at Birmingham.

A native of Birmingham, Alabama, Freeland currently resides in Pasadena, Maryland, with her husband, R. Gregory Freeland, president of FiHoldings Inc., and their twin daughters, Brya Simone and Brynn Nicole. They are also the proud parents of one deceased son, Richard Gregory II, for whom RGII Technologies Inc. was named.